The Pocket Essential

HAL HARTLEY

First published in Great Britain 2003 by
Pocket Essentials, P O Box 394, Harpenden, Herts, AL5 1XJ, UK

Distributed in the USA by Trafalgar Square Publishing,
PO Box 257, Howe Hill Road, North Pomfret, Vermont 05053

Copyright © Jason Wood 2003
Series Editor: David Mathew

A CIP catalogue record for this book is available from the British Library.

ISBN 1-904048-14-5

2 4 6 8 10 9 7 5 3 1

Book typeset by Wordsmith Solutions Ltd
Printed and bound by Cox & Wyman

For my son Felix.

Acknowledgements

For helping with materials: Will Clarke, Steve Jenkins and Alice Bruggen (the BBC), Myriad Pictures, Nick Jones (Channel 4), Linda Pariser, Ben Roberts, Robert Ryder (Barbican Cinema), and especially to Geoff Andrew, who kindly allowed access to his library of Hartley tapes. Appreciation is also extended to Eileen Anipare, Paul Duncan, Andy Jeyes and to my wife Nicky.

Note: Quotes have been taken from various sources. These are listed in the Reference Materials section at the back of the book.

CONTENTS

Introduction:
The Aesthetics Of Economy:
The Cinema Of Hal Hartley

Undoubtedly one of the most distinctive voices in contemporary American cinema, director Hal Hartley has continued to plough his own independent furrow, paying scant regard to cinematic fads and fashions or the dictates of dominant mainstream cinema. Imposing an idiosyncratic style and sensibility on established genres and conventions to give the impression that his films exist in a world almost entirely of their own, Hartley is a genuine candidate for auteur status. As director, writer, producer, editor and composer, in the latter category often under the humorous Ned Rifle moniker, a recurring *nom de plume*, he has amassed a phenomenally diverse and distinguished body of work that to date includes seven features (excluding the hour-long *The Book Of Life*) and numerous experimental shorter pieces. Teasing out the potentials of the medium to their fullest, there is the overriding impression that each of his films is part of a longer, continual work in progress in which his own capabilities as a director and his relationship to his spectators is constantly being challenged and redefined.

Born on November 3rd, 1959 in Islip, New York, Hartley grew up in Lindenhurst, a working-class commuter belt of Long Island. The environment in which Hartley spent his formative years was not only to act as a setting for his early output but also to have a lasting effect in his depiction of blue-collar lives and the struggle with the class and culture dichotomy. It also informed Hartley's own astute understanding of the dynamics between aesthetics and economy, instilling in the director a low-budget mindset that was to serve him well in a career founded on being creative on limited means. Initially studying painting at the Massachusetts College of Art in Boston during the academic year 1977-78, a subject that was to exert a profound and lasting influence in terms of his favouring of tableaux-like arrangements of figures and landscapes, Hartley began to develop an interest in film, making a number of Super 8mm shorts. In 1980 Hartley swapped painting for pictures, enrolling at the State University Of New York Purchase film school, studying under the director Aram Avakian. *Kid*, Hartley's graduation film contained numerous stylistic and thematic motifs that would later develop into an authorial signature, most notably perhaps a frustration with suburban small-town life, tersely spoken dialogue, a minimalist approach to *mise-en-scene* and a distinct, almost fastidious and Bressonian approach to framing and composition.

Following graduation, Hartley worked for a time with his father in the construction business as an apprentice ironworker and his work retains a respect for people who are adept at working manually with their hands. With his interest in cinema increasing and becoming more passionate and diverse, Hartley completed two more shorts, *The Cartographer's Girlfriend* and *Dogs*. The films helped solidify the fledgling director's interest in small town *ennui*, the tribulations of male-female relations, and a judicious approach to directing, while establishing what was to become an ongoing rapport with key cast and crew members, such as cinematographer and college alumni Michael Spiller and actress Karen Sillas. Hoping to precipitate a move into further directing assignments, Hartley worked in a freelance capacity on a number of commercials before taking a menial job answering phones for a Manhattan-based TV company that produced public-service announcements. It was a fortuitous appointment. Hartley's employer, Jerome Brownstein, was impressed by Hartley's three early shorts and agreed to fund his first feature to the tune of $75,000. *The Unbelievable Truth* more than delivered on the promise of Hartley's early film forays. As well as achieving a confident and irreverent fusion of stylisation, inventiveness and narrative lucidity, the film was heralded, along with Steven Soderbergh's *sex, lies and videotape* as being indicative of a new wave in low budget American independent filmmaking, maintaining a lineage between the work of independent iconoclasts such as John Cassavetes and John Sayles. With his similar irreverence for genre, Jim Jarmusch was served up by critics as an early point of reference, though the work of European modernists such as Jean-Luc Godard and Studio auteurs like Howard Hawks and Preston Sturges was much more discernible in Hartley's debut feature. A profound influence on future micro-budget directors such as Richard Linklater and, believe it or not, Kevin Smith, *The Unbelievable Truth* made a key virtue of its italicised, aphoristic, witty dialogue. As Hartley was quick to point out, talk is cheap when you're working on a tight budget.

Though working with marginally increased budgets on his next two features, *Trust* and *Simple Men*, and making minimal refinements in style, the director retained the inventiveness and economical approach to the construction of images and the efficient communication of meaning that he attributed to working within the confines of a tight budget. Part of a Long Island trilogy, though the final film, *Simple Men*, was shot partly in Texas, the films displayed a homogeneity both in terms of the director's continued association with a repertory group of cast and crew and through the ways in which the films playfully made reference to each other. This added to the work in progress sensibility and also suggested a director all too ready to engage with the sense of illusion essential to fictive cinema. Somewhat darker in tone than his first feature and shorn of the Godardian quirks – though professing his admiration for the director Hartley has been quick to downplay the influence – both *Trust* and *Simple Men* continued Hartley's examination of cloying, dysfunctional families and issues of trust in binding relationships. Shot in trademark bold, primary colours, the films also extended his observations on the mores of contemporary society. Perhaps most importantly, the films continued the director's interest in the perception of women and the ways in which men define their existence in terms of their dependences on them; Hartley's ability to create intelligent, feisty female characters was to remain a staple of his work. All three films tentatively suggested an interest in both the role that music of the diegetic and non-diegetic variety plays in cinema and how the juxtaposition of sound and image relates to meaning. In this regard the director's desire to allow his work to take a more experimental direction was implicitly revealed.

This desire to experiment and abandon the tyranny of conventional narrative arcs was brought to the fore in three short films that Hartley made between *Trust* and *Simple Men*. The first of these, *Theory Of Achievement,* looked at a bunch of disaffected Brooklyn dwellers struggling to bridge the gulf between the aspirations suggested by their college educations and the reality of their humdrum lives. Determinedly loose in structure, the film however retained the director's affection for witty and profound rapport between his characters and his favouring of detached, deadpan performances. *Ambition* was altogether more freeform and while also covering the theme of professional dissatisfaction, was perhaps most notable for expanding the director's interest in the synergy between movement, choreography and sound. Very much a precursor for Hartley's later shorts (and here his admiration for the liberating potentials of the short format must be stressed) the film also allowed the director's quizzical look at sudden outbursts of violence to rise to the fore, becoming more pronounced and menacing in a society becoming increasingly prone to acts of physical barbarism. In later works this barbarism would extend to the director's sketching of a society in complete disarray.

Surviving Desire, the final short from the period, was ostensibly something of a throwback to Hartley's earlier work. A seemingly conventional tale of love in bad faith that again suggested the director's love of literature and of having his characters recite from books, it again made a virtue of understated but revealing aphorisms such as 'knowing is not enough.' Dig deeper however and the film again reveals the director's desire to abandon traditional narrative arcs and incorporate music, movement and choreography into his work, as evidenced by the scene where the male protagonist breaks into an impromptu dance with two passers-by. Hartley would repeat the device in later works, also continuing his preoccupation with an onscreen discourse with elements of popular culture.

Amateur retained Hartley's favouring of off-kilter camera angles and his distrust of establishing shots, revealing a director prone to shoot scenes as if the spectator had looked in upon them mid-sentence. Similarly, the film revealed a filmmaker unafraid of letting the processes by which images are constructed show; the film begun with the image of Martin Donovan – by now an archetypal Hartley performer – that closed *Surviving Desire* and closed with what was the original ending of *Simple Men*. The film however favoured a more sombre palette to reflect the relocation to the streets of New York, the director's spiritual home. Working for the first time with a bona fide star, the legendary French actress Isabelle Huppert, and with a larger budget at his disposal, Hartley felt compelled to come up with something a little less esoteric and so hijacked the conventions of the thriller genre for the tale of the relationship between a violent pornographer suffering from amnesia and a would-be nymphomaniac ex-nun. In hijacking the conventions, and the film's title as much as anything refers to the position from which Hartley made the film, the director also subverted them, especially in his consideration of the ways in which we are conditioned to anticipate and react to onscreen gunplay. From the get-go, a socially aware, gently political director, *Amateur* saw Hartley engaging further with issues such as right wing politics, pornography and violence towards women. Reflecting his Catholic upbringing, religion had often appeared as a footnote in Hartley's films, here it was pushed further to the fore. Likewise, the emerging role of computer technology at the tail end of the 20th Century was another subject the film observed, a subject that was to become of regular interest to the director, specifically in his millennial drama *The Book Of Life*.

Hartley continued to explore and allowed his career to take in divergent forms and formats. Acclaimed for his pithy dialogue and his capacity to capture the rhythms and repetition of speech, Hartley wrote numerous plays, one of which, *Soon*, enjoyed the honour of being commissioned and staged at The Salzburg Opera Festival. A month later the play was performed in Antwerp and more recently in Orange County at the Orange County Performing Arts Center. As Hartley's skills as a composer had grown and music that utlisied classic forms began to appear in his work – Hartley is nothing if not culturally diverse – he also began to develop an interest in Opera and directed a short piece titled *Opera No.1*. As one might expect, it was an opera that incorporated the key elements of the medium but they were approached and incorporated in the director's own inimitable way.

From early in his career Hartley had forged lasting relationships with numerous and notable musicians and several times turned his hand to pop promos, producing videos for artists such as Everything But The Girl (*The Only Living Boy In New York* and *Walking Wounded*), Yo la Tengo (*From A Motel 6*), Masatoshi Nagase (*Boom N' Bust*) and Beth Orton (*Stolen Car*). Again the conventions of the medium were turned on their head, with the artists miming (Everything But The Girl's *The Only Living Boy In New York*) and the thrill of performance reduced to a setting up and the taking down of instruments (Yo La Tengo). Each promo Hartley has been involved with is in fact a perfectly achieved piece of work in its own right.

Hartley continued to revel in the liberties accorded him by the short format, often using his shorter pieces, a number of which were specially commissioned by art foundations across the world, particularly Europe where the director had accumulated a sizeable reputation, as a kind of celluloid laboratory in which he tried both new approaches to the art of directing and performance and emerging new technologies. Made prior to embarking upon *Amateur*, *Flirt NYC*, which was to later form part of the wider *Flirt* project was initially conceived of as a means of producing something on which the director could apply the basics of computer editing, a process he would be using on upcoming features. Similarly, other pieces such as *The Other Also* were shot using Digital Video technology, a format that afforded directors like Hartley the opportunity to work cheaply and with increased mobility. Keen to make the particular aesthetics of such technology a key part of the films as opposed to attempting to merely replicate the qualities of 35mm, an approach particularly evident in *The Book Of Life*, Hartley has recently come to work more and more in the short format. Both an aesthetic decision and part of the director's wish to continue to evolve as a director by testing out the grammar of filmmaking rather than merely reproducing his back catalogue, the move into shorter pieces was also the result of the changing marketplace and the tribulations of obtaining funding. In recognition of this new direction in which he wished to travel and his wish to pay less attention to the dictates of traditional film structure and production, Hartley recently re-named True Fiction Pictures, his long-standing production company under which he co-produced the majority of his work, Possible Films Incorporated. *Flirt*, Hartley's next feature was to prove one of the most significant moments in his career. A playful riff on the Jean Renoir inspired adage that every filmmaker really only ever remakes his or her first film, albeit with minor alterations – an observation negatively levelled at Hartley by his detractors – the film told the same story three times in different milieus, namely New York, Berlin and Tokyo, the latter cities also providing important sources of funding. Featuring lines of dialogue, situations and character 'types' repeated to varying dramatic and thematic effect, *Flirt* made transparent the art of creation, going so far as to have characters in the film comment on Hartley's failures and successes as a filmmaker. The Tokyo sequence even more clearly foregrounded the project's wish to consider how repetition and environment can create meaning, by including a performance by Hartley as none other than Hal Hartley. A potentially dry theoretical and philosophical exercise, it's an ultimately illuminating, enlightening and entertaining affair, leavened by the director's mischievous and self-deprecating sense of humour. On a personal level, the film, which offered an uncharacteristically unambiguous sense of closure, also introduced Hartley to his future wife, the actress Miho Nikaido.

Critically acclaimed and applauded for its formal risk-taking and open-ended discourse with its audience, *Flirt* however did not enjoy commercial success. The film's rigorous approach to structure and composition was repeated in shorter works such as *The New Math(s)* but Hartley found feature financing increasingly difficult to come by. Refusing to let funding issues alter his perceptions of his work or indeed his approach to filmmaking, Hartley was however finally forced to make *Henry Fool* for comparatively the same cost as his second feature. Demonstrating his ability to adapt to the environments surrounding production, Hartley produced perhaps his most epic and mature work to date. Expounding on recurring preoccupations such as the relationship between an experienced, culturally informed outcast (albeit in this instance between two males) and a younger initiate, the film also continued the exploration of the value artistic creation assumes in the media mediated marketplace. Like his previous features *Henry Fool* mined a dark terrain, revealing a brutish, violent society on the brink of implosion. The film also had fun confounding the expectations of critics and audiences alike, appropriating bawdy, overtly sexual imagery and dialogue as if to pay wry lip service to the fare popularly demanded by contemporary cinemagoers.

The aforementioned *The Book Of Life* was again a specially commissioned piece, in this instance by the French TV channel La Sept ARTE as part of a project that invited filmmakers from across the world to portray their thoughts on the significance of the dawning new millennium. A profound if contentious and highly personal re-imagining of Christ's arrival back on earth to judge the souls of the living and the dead, the film found the director fortifying creative relationships and returning to recurring concerns such as the role of religion, love and the failings and foibles of the human race. Shot through with characteristic wit and humility, the film revealed the extent to which Hartley was able to positively embrace digital technology to effectively mirror the role technology plays in shaping our lives on screen: The Book Of Life is in fact a laptop, whilst using the physical characteristics of the digital medium to beguiling and mesmeric effect.

The interest in genetics and a consideration of the very future of mankind is also reflected in the director's most recent work, *No Such Thing*, the tale of an alcoholic, insomniac monster (the film's original title) weary of humanity and of his own abject existence. Partly funded by Francis Ford Coppola's American Zoetrope company with further funding forthcoming from The Icelandic Film Corporation, the film sees Hartley once again balancing working with name actors, including Julie Christie and Helen Mirren whilst retaining performers that act as a kind of cinematic shorthand for the director's work: Robert John Burke, Damian Young and Bill Sage being just three examples. The cinematography, which juxtaposes the mean, city streets of New York with the rugged countryside of Iceland, retains the director's affection for filming in situations alien to him and is of course courtesy of Michael Spiller, who is as visually astute as ever, contributing some of his best work. Having previously purloined characteristics from genres such as the melodrama, the western, the musical and the thriller, *No Such Thing* finds Hartley dipping his toe into horror, science fiction and beauty and the beast mythology. For the first time Hartley grapples with the artifices of special effects, but he does so in his own incomparable manner, mainly to further the metaphorical device of having a fire-breathing ogre as a central character. *No Such Thing* continues the consideration of the manipulatory role of the media evidenced in *Henry Fool*, retaining particular ire for a Fox-style TV network company that makes entertainment out of human suffering and tragedy. Post September 11th, the film's referencing to terrorist attacks on both New York and the world in general makes for portentous viewing.

No Such Thing continued the tradition Hartley had enjoyed of having his films premiered at the prestigious Cannes Film Festival. Its reception however was, in contrast to previous approbation distinctly muted, a response the film has for the most part continued to draw. This reaction perhaps reveals more about the expectations of critics and to a lesser extent audiences (the reaction from the public to the film in the States has been more positive) who seem to be willing the director to return to the formula offered in his formative, to quote Woody Allen's *Stardust Memories* 'early funny' movies. Hartley is not a director who adheres to formulas and moreover, this attitude seemingly overlooks the deceptively polemical nature of the first features.

Though it would perhaps be disingenuous to place the admittedly flawed but nonetheless engrossing *No Such Thing* amongst the director's finest achievements (there are reports of a troubled post-production), to believe that Hartley has to any extent suffered a loss of confidence or direction is an attitude that does a disservice to the uncompromising and disparate body of work Hartley has amassed in his relatively short career. A practitioner of refinement, freedom of expression and progression, Hartley has tackled new forms, formats and indeed existing approaches to filmmaking with a refreshing vigour, an omnipresent depth and an unnerving lack of inhibition. At the time of writing teaching in Cambridge, Massachusetts, Hartley's next move should be anticipated with fervour.

The Early Shorts

Hartley began making Super 8mm films whilst studying painting at the Massachusetts College of Art, Boston. The three shorts in this chapter are recognised as being the earliest examples of his work. As well as representing Hartley's affection for the liberating potentials of the short format, a format to which he would increasingly return to rid himself of the constrictions of narrative fiction, the three films also tentatively reveal numerous thematic and aesthetic preoccupations that would pepper his work and introduce us to cast and crew members who were to become regular collaborative figures. As they are shorter, formative pieces I have refrained from giving a grading.

Kid (1984)

Cast: Ricky Ludwig (Ned), Leo Gosse (Ned's Father), Janine Erickson (accordion girl), Karen Sillas (Patsy), Bob Gosse (Bruce), George Feaster (Ivan), Pamela Stewart (Ivan's sister), David Troup (the boyfriend).

Crew: Direction Hal Hartley, Screenplay Hal Hartley, Cinematography Michael Spiller, Music Hal Hartley, Editor Hal Hartley, 33 minutes.

Story: Desperate to leave the confines of Lindenhurst and small town life to go in search of his girlfriend in the city, Ned finds himself tethered to his hometown by his dependent father's apron strings, the attentions of deranged women and their brutish boyfriends, the cloying needs of friends and finally the affections of his savvy young sister (the 'kid' of the title). Finally, Ned makes for the train station but in a scene that rekindles *Billy Liar*, ultimately opts to return home with his father.

Style: Shooting on 16mm colour stock with Michael Spiller in his hometown of Lindenhurst, *Kid* was Hartley's graduation film. Obviously influenced by constrictive funds (the colour stock lends the film a somewhat grainy quality that is in fact highly effective) it certainly inspired in the director an economic approach to filmmaking both in terms of narrative and shooting style with much of the action, including a car accident involving a bicycle being fastidiously choreographed. Hartley's sense of composition already seems well formed; there's an abstract positioning of characters within the frame, as does a favouring of aphoristic dialogue that seems to mirror characters' subconscious fears and yearnings. Hartley also displays an early awareness of the possibilities of sound/image juxtaposition, using choral accompaniment and static radio sound bursts to accompany Ivan's rallying speech against the conformity of small town life.

Subtext: Kid can be seen as an embryonic encapsulation of many of the themes to which Hartley would consistently return (the director himself described it as 'a discussion about wanting to escape.' (1): disaffection with small town existence (one character asserts when hearing of Ned's plans to leave 'you've got the right idea, nothing's happening here'), fraught parental relations, the elusiveness of love and the forging of and the search for personal identity. Moreover, *Kid* also contains the seeds of Hartley's fascination with sudden violent eruptions such as frequent punches, shoves and slaps and equally unannounced amorous outbursts, as when Ivan's sister kisses Ned full on the mouth.

Verdict: An impressive work and a valuable indicator of what was to follow. *Kid* also displays an astute visual awareness and picks out some arresting imagery, not least the scene of the kid playing on deserted railway tracks.

The Cartographer's Girlfriend (1987)

Cast: Marissa Chibas (Girl), Steven Geiger (Boy), George Feaster (George), Lorraine Achee (Mom), Robert Richmond (Dad), Karen Sillas, David Troup.

Crew: Direction Hal Hartley, Screenplay Hal Hartley, Cinematography Michael Spiller, Production Design Carla Gerona, Music Hal Hartley, Editor Hal Hartley, 29 minutes.

Story: A young, suburban dwelling surveyor (Bob) working for the city finds his obsession with cartography challenged when he falls into a sudden, torrid physical relationship with a beautiful and enigmatic girl. The affair places further strain on the man's already fraught relationship with his parents. The advice of a chauvinistic, would-be womanising colleague who believes that Bob should take all the wanton sex he can only leads to further confusion and inner turmoil. Finally, the relationship is unsustainable and the woman flees to the city.

Style: Again shot in Lindenhurst on 16mm colour by Michael Spiller, the film seems much more confidant than its predecessor and has a lighter touch and feel, specifically within the white-washed walls of the airy apartment Bob shares with his parents. The colours are crisper, adding to a more distinct visual style. The meticulous sense of composition remains very much in evidence, as is Hartley's pronounced use of the way in which he places his actors within the frame, often to accentuate other objects or indeed other frames, such as doors, windows etc. In many ways, the precision of the cartographer of the title matches the filmmaker's acute, pared down visual aesthetic.

Subtext: The enigmatically titled and presented *The Cartographer's Girlfriend* is again redolent of later work; most specifically perhaps *Trust* in its hero's confused relationship with a beautiful, independent woman and the presence of meddling, non-communicative parents. The film demonstrates Hartley's witty aptness to reference literature and popular culture, showing the mysterious woman reading a trash novel (*Triangle Of Lust*) and a discussion about love set to a TV re-run of an old western. The latter scene again offers early evidence of Hartley's approach to dialogue and his motif of having his characters speak-out loud their inner feelings, often with candid honesty, insight (tinged with a despair at the anxiety of love) but also gentle humour: 'all women look alike because when a man's in love he can't see a thing.' More playful than *Kid*, the film also signals the emergence of Hartley's interest in the more base nature of male friendships and camaraderie with Bob's colleague dispensing advice predicated purely on sexual considerations. Drunk, thumbing pornography, another subject frequently covered, the two men are later seen puking into an empty bathtub after a sexually confident woman (Karen Sillas) accepts an invitation to 'hey baby, make my dreams come true.'

Verdict: Perhaps the best of Hartley's early work – the balance between stylisation, naturalism and irony sits just right – and a film that strangely reminds of a blue collar *Last Tango In Paris*, with added tenderness. Admirers of the first three features and *Surviving Desire* will find much to applaud here.

Dogs (1988)

Cast: Ricky Ludwig, Mike Brady, Gary Sauer.

Crew: Direction Hal Hartley, Screenplay Hal Hartley, Steven O'Connor, Richard Ludwig, based on a portion from Eugene O'Neill's *The Iceman Cometh*, Cinematography Steven O'Connor, Production Design Liz Hazan, Editor Steven O'Connor, 20 minutes.

Story: Dogs examines the aftermath of a riotous night out of a trio of men, one of whom is returning to his hometown after making good in the city and marrying the town beauty. As frustration, jealousy and small-town *ennui* rise to the fore, it is revealed that the supposed idyllic existence of the returning hero is a veneer: his marriage is a never-ending series of infidelities and his high flying job is actually a blue collar post on a production line. Finally, the man confesses to his astonished suburbanites that he has murdered his sleeping wife, unable to accept the unquestioning affection she has shown him.

Style: The film takes an experimental, metaphorical approach to editing, juxtaposing the latent aggression of the men with colour-saturated (the film was shot on Super-8 colour) images of savage, snarling dogs. Hartley's sense of composition is again acute and in one scene he has one character walking towards a sign reading 'Dead End'. Moreover, characters are often shot from above in a tableaux-like effect with one shot of the three men head by head with a bicycle wheel mirroring a similar shot from *The Unbelievable Truth.* The later gutter images of Martin Donovan *Surviving Desire* and *Amateur* also come to mind.

Subtext: Dogs expands upon the suffocating nature of small town life and mores and to a lesser degree male/female relationships and sexual jealousy. More keenly observed here is the aggressiveness that develops between men and the initially playful banter that soon develops darker, more violent overtones. The violence is not merely absurdist; it simmers somewhat viciously here, constantly threatening to come to the boil.

Verdict: An undoubtedly interesting work, especially in the way it contrasts with the other two films, if not a wholly successful one. Working from an updating of *The Iceman Cometh* the film never attempts to portray its three, boorish misogynistic protagonists in a sympathetic light but there is still an unpleasant coldness to the film and the repeated dog analogies finally feel a little laboured.

The Unbelievable Truth (1989)

Cast: Adrienne Shelly (Audry Hugo), Robert Burke (Josh Hutton), Christopher Cooke (Vic Hugo), Julia McNeal (Pearl), Mark Bailey (Mike), Gary Sauer (Emmet), Katherine Mayfield (Liz Hugo), David Healy (Todd Whitbread).

Crew: Direction Hal Hartley, Screenplay Hal Hartley, Cinematography Michael Spiller, Production Design Carla Gerona, Music Jim Coleman, Phillip Reed, Wild Blue Yonder, The Brothers Kendall, Editing Hal Hartley, 90 minutes.

Story: After years in prison Josh Hutton returns to Lindenhurst to resume his life. Unfortunately, the first person he runs into is Pearl, the sister of the girl whose death he caused. Josh's return precipitates widespread rancor and fans the flames of rumour concerning the details of the murder and his complicity in the death of other members of Pearl's family.

Meanwhile, Audry, a precocious teenager with an aversion to higher education and a belief in the impending threat of nuclear destruction is in the throes of ending her relationship with Emmet, her materialistic, self-obsessed boyfriend. Audry's father, Vic, is desperate for Audry to attend college but baulks at the idea of footing the bill for her preferred Harvard education. A deal between father and daughter is tentatively reached. A shared interest in George Washington brings Josh and Audry together, lifting Audry's pessimism concerning the future of the universe as she experiences a rush of affection for the enigmatic stranger. Aware that he is looking for work, Audry arranges employment at the garage owned by her father and Josh soon proves his worth as a mechanic, winning the respect of co-worker and Pearl's lover, Mike. However, as news of the simmering romance reaches Vic he threatens to fire his new charge unless Audry agrees to never see him again. A new deal is reached that allows Audry to see Josh one more time but her clumsy play for his attentions is rejected. Chastened, Audry embarks on a lucrative modelling career under the tutelage of a sleazy local photographer. Relocated to New York, Audry commands top dollar for modelling assignments, much to the chagrin of the folks back home who are quick to condemn her decision to pose naked for a shoot.

Humiliated in public on publication of the snaps, Vic hatches a plan to bring Josh and Audry back together and dispatches Josh to the city. Mistakenly believing that Audry is having an affair with the photographer, Josh smashes her window with a book on George Washington and returns to Lindenhurst. A teetotaler (it emerges that he killed Pearl's sister in a drink-driving accident) whose abstinence has led many to believe that he is a priest, Josh hits the bottle hard but is jerked back to sobriety when Pearl reveals the full extent of his involvement in the death of her father. The relief is short lived as the denizens of Lindenhurst descend upon Josh's house and accuse him of bedding Pearl.

As the confusion lifts, Audry annuls all her deals and embraces Josh. The pair prepare to hit the road, but overhead the sounds of war ominously appear.

Background: Any low budget production – certainly post-*Sundance* and the success of *sex, lies and videotape* – that goes on to prick the critical and public consciousness is apt to accrue a certain mythology concerning its background production and *The Unbelievable Truth* is no exception. Following the completion of *The Cartographer's Girlfriend* and *Dogs* Hartley had gone to work for a TV company that produced public service announcements and his idiosyncratic shorts obviously caught the eye of his boss, Jerome Brownstein, who agreed, no doubt with a little cajoling, to finance *The Unbelievable Truth* to the tune of $75,000. Hartley has often professed himself to be a tyrant of textual economy, little wonder given the modest means with which he returned to the hometown environs of Lindenhurst (with longstanding creative collaborators such as Michael Spiller, Carla Gerona and Gary Sauer in tow) to begin filming his debut feature and it is worth taking into account the way in which his style, and specifically his reliance on dialogue, was a direct result of the limited economic funds at his disposal. Moreover, Hartley's relatively blue-collar background had given him a low budget mindset and instilled in him the discipline and creativity to meet the challenge of producing something from limited financial means.

Style: Though Lindenhurst serves as the relatively innocuous background setting; the film is anything but mundane or drab in terms of its visual style. Former college alumni Michael Spiller's crisp, cinematography, complemented by Carla Gerona's equally spruce, unfussy production design, favours lush primary colours and in several tableaux-like sequences Hartley's art background is brought strikingly to the fore. The opening sequences, edited with a precision and disdain for the superfluous that perhaps acts as the overriding defining visual feature of the director's work are simply stunning. Particularly arresting, 'painterly' and typical of Hartley's acute sense of composition and awareness of the human form in relation to the environment is the medium long-shot (unusual as the film is largely defined by claustrophobic medium shots or close-up's) where we see the car driven by the down-on-his luck Otis (Matt Molloy) speed into view as Josh – fore grounded by rustling reeds -attempts to hitch a ride. This single specific image reminds of Terrence Malick, as a whole, the film bears more than a passing resemblance to the detailed if somewhat detached work of the painter Edward Hopper. In contrast, Hartley also utilizes numerous slightly off-kilter camera angles (a bored Audry floating across the pool on the lilo – evocative of *The Graduate;* Pearl and Audry in contemplative discussion after their midnight bicycle ride) to render the ordinary unfamiliar and no doubt to signal his own approach to the conventions and language of cinema.

Hartley's use of sound (something to which he has always paid particular attention) is equally unconventional. When we first see Audry she is waking in her bed; as she stretches we hear the sound of an explosion, an ominous portent of what perhaps lies ahead. As well as externalizing dialogue, i.e. having characters directly speak their innermost thoughts, the director is apt to do all kinds of weird and wonderful things with sound and dialogue, such as loop it and generally explore its formal and metaphorical possibilities. The bicycle scene is a good example; played out to a simplistic piece of music, we recognise that Audry and Pearl are in conversation but we are denied hearing their words.

There's a distinct lack of establishing shots (something Hartley has declared his disinterest in) with scenes often beginning as if in mid-flow, giving the sense that we have interrupted an already advanced, catalytic moment but been spared any superfluous build up. Once again, Hartley cuts to the quick. The director often propels the narrative through a series of jump cuts, most notably in the sequence where Vic repeatedly rips out the pages of the magazine in which his daughter has appeared nude. Stylistically the film does not bear the hallmarks of naturalism.

Hartley is however at pains to have fun with the various processes of the medium and the film is beautifully undercut with a formal playfulness. Throughout, Hartley punctuates the narrative and plugs the ellipses with concise, irreverent intertitles: 'Meanwhile', 'After a while', 'But', etc, as if to remind us that we are watching a piece of fiction and of the tyranny of sequential order. Moreover, the film is underpinned by a general humour, including the undeniably excessive physical outbursts and the slaps and shoves that would increase as Hartley's career progressed, here largely used to signify the base, possessive nature of men. Most successful of these moments is the scene where Emmet, who since being dumped by Audry because he 'disgusts' her, finally gets a chance to make her jealous by cavorting with another female (to the sound of jungle drums) before breaking off to shove and push a bystander (Bill Sage) who passes Audry admiring glances. Other excessive modes of behaviour include the increasingly complicated deals Audry makes with her father concerning her education and Vic's confession that his besotted daughter sleeps with Josh's wrench. The dialogue is genuinely funny (witness the constant assertions that Josh must be a priest), not least in the interactions between Mike and Josh concerning the need to brush up on physical hygiene once a female is on the scene and their none too subtle discussions of sexuality that reveal a conformist small town mentality, summarized by Mike's 'I used to think I was a homo. I joined the marines and they straightened my shit right out.'

Subtext: The film is equally rich thematically, but is perhaps most overtly concerned with the *ennui* and mindset of small-town life. In this, as well as in the gentle references to religion (Audry asserts that she wishes to be a carpenter because Jesus was one) and the blue-collar professions pursued by the characters (the film focuses upon mechanics and fixers and the director has also long professed an admiration for those that are capable of working with their hands) it is easy to see how Hartley's Lindenhurst background influenced the film. The small town mindset is evidenced in various ways: the increasingly hysterical tales and rumours surrounding Josh's background, who as the straight as a dye, honest outsider finally acts as a catalyst for truth, the sense of public humiliation suffered by Vic and Emmet, the jealousy that greets Audry's success and Vic's desire for his daughter to go off and better herself, but at no great expense to himself. The final example highlights another thematic concern: the corrupting nature of money, also evident in the manner in which Audry's ambitions are consumed by her growing bank balance.

The series of complicated deals that people make with each other signifies the lack of trust that exists and the sense that people will enter into a relationship only if they can expect some kind of kickback in return. Audry asserts, 'You can't have faith in people, only in the deals you make with them,' and at the end of the film, Josh states that he doesn't trust anyone, a theme that would go on to be explored in *Trust*. On a larger scale, *The Unbelievable Truth* is preoccupied with the problematic machinations of relationships, familial (the Hugo's display all the symptoms of a dysfunctional family and their attempts at communication and solidarity breakdown at ever turn), platonic and sexual, and as with much of the director's work features at its core a man and a woman both tentatively reaching out for each other as they move towards self-knowledge and a deeper individual consciousness. Interestingly, both Josh and Audry are keen readers and it is something of a motif in Hartley's work to have characters quote aloud from literature. A neat little touch here is to have Audry read from a book titled *The End Of The World* written by Ned Rifle. A whole chapter could be devoted to Ned. The lead character in *Kid*, the name was to crop up constantly in the director's work, most notably as the pseudonym under which Hartley composed his scores. Ned Rifle originated as an imagined character in a western when Hartley was studying at SUNY. Another factor linking Josh and Audry is their shared interest in George Washington, first glimpsed in a statue in the beginning of the film and later as a dollar bill on Audry's wall. Prior to the film Hartley had been writing a script about a man visited by the ghosts of George Washington and Benjamin Franklin and appropriated the theme because 'the juxtaposition of what George Washington popularly represents with his story of emotional commerce seemed appropriate.' (2)

A director who claims to 'deal with politics in human terms rather than dealing with humans in political terms' (3), *The Unbelievable Truth* certainly has a political bent, both in the way the film, with its independent, strong-willed lead female character (the creation of such types being another facet of Hartley's films), examines notions of exploitation (Audry is initially exploited by the predatory local photographer but then exploits him and her own physical assets into the bargain) but more pertinently in its alarmingly pessimistic views on the threat of nuclear war. Hartley himself as described the ending of the film, which typically avoids a neat resolution, as in part a trade-off between Josh's optimism and Audry's pessimism but also admits that at the time of the film's making it would have been somewhat 'naive to assume atomic bombs won't destroy the world.' (4)

Key Moment: A beautifully composed medium close-up (with sunlight breaking in from a nearby window), the scene takes place between Josh and a would-be suitor, Jane, (Edie Falco of *The Sopranos* fame) in the local diner following Josh's bust-up with the newly moneyed Audry.

Jane: 'I know what you need.'

Josh: 'Excuse me?'

Jane: 'You need a woman. That girl is crazy.'

Josh: 'I know but I like her a lot.'

Jane: 'But she's leaving town.'

Josh: 'So I hear.'

Jane: 'So come on, what'd ya say? I know what you need.'

Repeated with little variation in enunciation three times in succession, it's a moment that perfectly encapsulates Hartley's incisive approach to deadpan performance, the construction and rhythm of dialogue: namely his having his characters simply speak their inner thoughts out loud without contemplation of social niceties, and his willingness to make repetition a virtue.

Music: Working with regular Jim Coleman and guitarist Phillip Reed, the template was set for the music that would help define Hartley's early features. The incidental music is primarily of the lo-fi rock variety and incorporates lyrically sensitive, mournful but altogether guitar heavy songs about the impossibility of love to fine effect. A sustained guitar chord or synthesizer note often underscores a physical or emotional outburst. It is also worth noting that Hartley, perhaps looking ahead to *Surviving Desire* and his ambition to film a rock band performing, has Mike as a guitar player, filming him numerous times as he runs through a series of increasingly outlandish riffs.

Verdict: The Unbelievable Truth set in motion Hartley's crafting of a body of work that has continued to resist easy categorisation, existing in a particular genre all of its own. Ostensibly a small town drama about an enigmatic, potential mass murderer finding love, *The Unbelievable Truth* also borrows from the western - a genre Hartley studied at film school - (the returning stranger), the Restoration farce (the final beach house scene where the town members accidentally come together, miss each other and generally breed suspicion and confusion), and the issue-based drama (the impending threat of nuclear destruction) to witty if elusive effect. Various influences can be discerned in the work; European modernists such as Godard, Studio-era craftsmen like Howard Hawks and Frank Capra but perhaps the overriding feeling one gets from re-watching the film (back in 1989 it certainly felt like a breath of fresh air though Jim Jarmusch was the oft-quoted point of reference) is the distinctive, decidedly indefinable originality it contains. The film inspired a new generation of cine-literate, dialogue driven directors such as Richard Linklater and is not only a stylish and confidant debut but remains one of the finest and archetypal U.S indie pics. 4/5.

Trust (1990)

Cast: Adrienne Shelly (Maria Coughlin), Martin Donovan (Matthew Slaughter), Rebecca Nelson (Jean Coughlin), John MacKay (Jim Slaughter), Edie Falco (Peg Coughlin), Gary Sauer (Anthony), Karen Sillas (Nurse Paine).

Crew: Direction Hal Hartley, Screenplay Hal Hartley, Cinematography Michael Spiller, Production Design Daniel Ouellette, Music Phillip Reed, The Great Outdoors, Editing Nick Gomez, 106 minutes.

Story: Maria Coughlin's announcement that she is pregnant and dropping out of school has a devastating effect on her suburban family. After casting his 'sluttish' daughter from the family bosom, Maria's father suffers, unbeknownst to his errant daughter, a fatal heart attack. Meanwhile, Matthew Slaughter, a fiery 'genius' with an aversion to TV and a love of classical music and literature, quits his job at a computer plant due to their failure to respect and match his idealism and high standards.

Returning home to his abusive, order-obsessed father (it transpires that he suffered the loss of his wife during his son's birth), Matthew is castigated for his actions and similarly ejected. Armed with the hand-grenade he carries as a symbol of his self-destructive bent, Matthew seeks solace, stumbling across a drunken Maria, reeling from the loss of her father, the realization that her jock boyfriend Anthony is a self-obsessed chauvinist and a near-molestation experience from the local liquor-store owner. Needing a place to sleep, Maria returns home with Matthew but is subsequently humiliated by Matthew's father and the pair again flee; Matthew to a bar where he physically abuses other drinkers before spurning the attentions of Peg, a divorced mother of two who just happens to be Maria's sister. Matthew returns home with Maria and Peg but the homecoming is not a happy one as Jean, the pairs' mother vows to enslave Maria in retribution for her husband's death.

Awed by Matthew's intellect and principled ways, the increasingly bookish Maria develops a thirst for knowledge and vows to get her life back on track, taking a menial job to pay off her debts and pave the way for college education. A search for a kidnapped child that leads to a frustrated, grief-stricken woman trapped in a loveless marriage causes romance to blossom, resulting in Matthew's proposal and a swallowing of his pride when he returns to his humdrum job.

Taking a dim view of the romance, Jean attempts to sabotage the relationship, forcing Peg and Matthew together. Believing that he has betrayed her, Maria has an abortion and confronts Matthew – who after having to kowtow to inferiors again quits his job – with the truth that she does not wish to marry him. Distraught, Matthew heads back to the plant with his grenade, failing to take his own life but causing mass destruction. Bundled into a police car and whisked off to jail, his disappearance into the distance is watched by the re-awakened Maria, sporting the 'librarian's' glasses Matthew was so fond of.

Background: The Unbelievable Truth had established Hartley's name and so he was fortunate enough to not have to rely upon the kindness of employers for his next project. Financed by British production outfit Zenith in conjunction with Film Four and Hartley's newly formed True Fiction Pictures (a production company Hartley still oversees to this day), *Trust* saw the director working with a larger budget. In the grand scheme of production costs, $650,000 is still small potatoes but an improvement nonetheless on the $75,000 the director had at his disposal for his debut. Maintaining his preference for economy and what can perhaps be described as a judicious, minimalist approach in terms of style, Hartley and cinematographer Michael Spiller again ventured onto the streets of Lindenhurst for what, on paper, appears to be a slightly skewed small-town boy meets girl melodrama.

Style: Opening mid-family meltdown with a series of close-up's on the faces of the fractious Coughlin family (the film is again distinctive in its use of colour, with white and subtle pastel shades defining the film, especially the interior sequences), we are aware from the very first frame that this is a Hal Hartley film. As well as echoing the director's distrust of establishing shots, the encounter also signifies Hartley's highly stylized and signature positioning of figures within the frame. Details of faces are picked out with the presence of other characters indicated purely by off-camera voices. Hartley seems as interested in what others may feel to be minor details as he is in capturing portentous actions. Thus, the slap Maria delivers that precipitates her father's heart attack though evident in the frame is more readily signified through the expression on the face of her mother Jean.

Matthew shot from above in his room when his grenade is first revealed and the perfectly achieved aerial head shots of Matthew and Maria post explosion are prime examples of Hartley's utilisation of oblique angles and often jarring close-ups. This approach to framing seems influenced as much by painting, intricate tableaux-like compositions are again evident throughout, as by anything in contemporary cinema. The shot of the appropriately named Matthew Slaughter after quitting his job purposefully striding past

26

an elaborate fusion of pylons and overhead industrial cables not only connotes the character's complicated, confused nature but again stresses the director's often stunning juxtaposition of his characters with their environment. Also of note in this regard is the end of the film. Wholly in keeping with Hartley's avoidance of crowd-pleasing closure for more honest and ambiguous conclusions, the camera captures Slaughter's hang-dog expression as he is whisked away into the distance to a lengthy and unpleasant imprisonment eyed by a purposeful, re-focused Maria positioned at a metaphorical and literal crossroads. Visually astute and in itself pleasurable, the image also reveals Maria, purposefully donning spectacles, seeing things clearly for the very first time. Maria's future seems filled with options; Matthew's less so.

Before returning to other formal concerns, it's worth noting the minor feminist icon Hartley created in *Trust* and the director's creation of and focus upon strong-willed female characters which not only take center-stage in terms of narrative but who also act as catalysts for internal and external change. As in *The Unbelievable Truth*, the female character (again wonderfully played by Adrienne Shelly and written by Hartley as the kind of character 'I wanted to see' (5)) goes through a period of renewed self-awareness, personal development and growth, emerging from sullen, self-obsession to independence and maturity. Finally freeing herself from the tyranny of a patriarchal society willing to exploit her sex at every turn, Maria comes to exist on her own terms, rejecting the dim future of early motherhood, a marriage of convenience and a meager existence of bad T.V, alcoholism, shopping and housework all too easily taken by her contemporaries (sister Peg included). The limited options available to the town's female denizens are clearly presented in a tenderly written scene in which members of the Coughlin family and a pal of Peg's discuss life pre and post divorce and the tribulations of early pregnancy.

Perhaps more discrete than its predecessor in terms of its editing structure (gone are the intertitles) *Trust* nonetheless takes an almost determinedly non-naturalistic stance. The montage sequence where Matthew repeatedly cleans and re-cleans the gleaming white bathroom at the behest of his hygiene obsessed father (the vigor with which Matthew is expected to perform this role suggests the blame he must carry for his mother's death) is wonderfully composed of very quick, jump-cuts. Overall, the dominant feeling is of a director who wishes to communicate ideas and images quickly with the eradication of any non-essential material.

The venting of aggression in violent, short staccato bursts is retained as a stylistic motif. In fact, Martin Donovan has accrued something of a reputation with admirers of Hartley's work eager to see him deliver a blow or slap to an unsuspecting victim. Slaughter does this on numerous occasions, placing his supervisor's head in a vice, unwittingly delivering retribution by punching out Maria's would-be molester in a bar and grappling with a man in an abortion clinic waiting room. It's worth noting that these moments of slapstick (and there are numerous others, each more absurd) feature performances by two regular Hartley actors (Matt Malloy and Bill Sage) with other regulars such as Karen Sillas, M.C Bailey, and Gary Sauer filling out roles. The continual re-appearance of a regular band of longstanding actors contributed from the get-go to the sense of an authorial signature and homogeneity to the work.

Hartley has mentioned that he likes to have fun with the foolish side of men and these moments of violence, though containing an underlying seriousness, certainly do that. *Trust* maintains its sense of humour in other ways too from the ridiculousness of the blandness of the *Cape Holiday* commuters and the farcical detective work undertaken to locate one of their members to the typically witty and perceptive dialogue. The talk is cheap maxim is again in evidence and Hartley certainly makes a virtue of his talents as a writer. There's a sprinkling of earthy one-liners (Matthew's father accuses him of thinking that he 'shits ice cream cones') and the continued trend of having characters speak their minds aloud (Maria's reaction when Matthew shows her his grenade is an incredulous 'are you emotionally disturbed?'). There is however also real depth and a sense of the profound at play in the dialogue with often painful and uncomfortable truths and observations revealed to often disquieting effect. The woman who has kidnapped the young child quite shockingly reveals to Maria that not only has her own died but also that she hates her husband, who is 'absurdly like a little boy' and wishes her house would burn down. Just as the deceptively minimalist style reveals hidden depths, in many ways the dialogue is also representative of Hartley's desire to explore painful themes and social issues and is, as a result more direct and less elliptical than that in *The Unbelievable Truth*; it's also more profane.

Subtext: The agonizing over the concept of trust in Hartley's debut feature again recurs. As a test Matthew is forced to catch Maria as she falls from a great height but recoils when expected to repeat the feat with Maria as the buffer. Interestingly, Hartley conspires to ensure that the act of falling is not repeated but one can't help but feel, especially given the outcome of the relationship, that the director is not too convinced of the foundations of the relationship nor of the capacity for trust between people in general. He does however leave us with a handy equation (Matthew and Maria barter over it, again illustrating the director's interesting observation that even intimate relationships are based on deals); 'respect, trust and admiration equals love.'

Given the setting of the film and the troubled relationships contained therein, it's easy to discern other concerns that again crop up from Hartley's earlier work: the stifling nature and enforced conformity of small-town existence (shots of trains to other more exciting destinations often feature), the unappealing nature of family life and the overweening role of parents, abusive relationships, journeys to a clearer consciousness, environmental issues (Matthew expresses concern for the ozone layer), the weight of the past (Matthew has spent time in psychiatric institutions and his capacity for rage is a genuine illness) and the thirst for learning and appreciation of culture readily to come mind. Incidentally, it's worth again noting the director's fondness for having books appear in his work and the presenting of the dichotomy between an appreciation for cultural pursuits opposed to working class ideals and concerns. The Ned Rifle connection again occurs with Maria reading from a book by Rifle titled *Man And The Universe*. As a final adjunct, Hartley again displays his admiration for people who can fix things; Jim Slaughter may slam his son's head against a fridge door but he knows how to get an engine running.

Hartley's willingness to cover disturbing issues in his work is an often-overlooked asset and *Trust* certainly finds him engaging with some of the darker aspects of society. On the release of *Henry Fool* Ryan Gilbey penned an article praising Hartley for abandoning the perceived frivolity of earlier work for something that reflected the impinging harshness of reality but I would argue that the director has always incorporated the brutality of the world around him. Premature death and a sense of lives wasted winds its way constantly through the film and there's also the kidnapping and abduction of a young child to contend with. Further, there are the aforementioned issues surrounding teenage pregnancies and under-age sex. Picking up on the debate surrounding abortion (anti-abortion protestors picket the clinic Maria visits), Hartley delivers a sobering, measured argument concerning the right to choose. The exploitation of and objectification of women is dealt with candor and directness, most poignantly in the moment when Maria realises what Anthony had seen in her, 'he's seeing my legs, my breasts, my ass...he's seeing my cunt.' Likewise, in dealing with violence against women Hartley pulls no punches and the sequence where the beer-seller takes Maria outback to assault her is genuinely disturbing.

The general tone of the film is one of abject longing, loneliness and unhappiness. Without exception the characters have not only compromised their ideals but more poignantly suffered profound loss and regret and are involved in the daily struggle of coming to terms with their respective disappointments and grief. Matthew's loss of freedom at the film's close is an apt metaphor for the pervading sense of imprisonment throughout.

Key Moment: Steadfast in his refusal to watch television ('it gives you cancer'), the dexterous Matthew emerges from the flirtatious Peg's room after fixing hers. He meets Maria who is preparing for bed. After educating her on the meaning of the word empirical, the pair move into an intimate close-up. In a subdued, seductive bluish light, Maria reveals her dislike of wearing glasses because they make her look like a librarian. 'I like librarians' deadpans Matthew and to the backdrop of the melodic score the seeds of romance are sown.

The scene works well not only in terms of the various compositional elements and the chemistry between Donovan and Shelly (Hartley's abilities as a director of actors should not be forgotten) but because it exists in stark opposition to the ensuing sadness. An unashamedly romantic interlude, future happiness for the pair is provocatively suggested. Of course, reality rears its ugly head and after having to 'subvert his principles' and take his job back, Matthew is soon reduced to necking beers on the sofa, engrossed in a medium that 'deadens the core of his being.'

Music: Hartley's ear for incorporating a fine guitar ditty is gloriously intact with two The Great Outdoors tracks written by Hub Moore, *Walk Away* and the rousing *Mess With Me*, incorporated to harmonious and highly appropriate effect. Commonly and mistakenly associated with soundtracks that rely solely on the inclusion of songs from the rock idiom, no doubt due to Hartley's own association and fondness for some of the finer U.S artists of the genre, the music in *Trust* gives early evidence of the divergence at play. Phillip Reed's synthesized, bittersweet score perfectly captures the melancholic, mournful environment inhabited by the characters whilst the use of classical music reflects not only Matthew Slaughter's cultured palate but also the director's willingness to draw from varied and esoteric sources.

Verdict: Often described in terms of genre, not altogether unfavorably, as containing the characteristics of a daytime soap, *Trust* is on the most superficial of levels an intelligent melodrama – stripped of all Sirkian excess –

given an irreverent spin. Perhaps less immediately likeable than *The Unbelievable Truth* and harder hitting in terms of subject matter and its depiction of the hardships of reality, it marks a very clear progression in Hartley's career as a writer. The witty aphorisms and ironic interactions remain intact but there's also a growing sense of Hartley using his gift for dialogue as less of a by-product of budgetary constraints and as more of a virtue and means of directness in their own right. Needless to say, Hartley's distinctive visual aesthetic is evidenced throughout and the film feels less detached and stylistically less self-conscious than its predecessor. Confirmation, if it were needed, of an important new voice in contemporary American cinema. 4/5.

The Middle Shorts

In 1991, during the interim period between *Trust* and *Simple Men* Hartley made three shorts for American public television. Two of them, *Theory Of Achievement* and *Ambition* were for the *Alive From Off Center* arts series, the third, *Surviving Desire* – the longest and most conventional of the three – was produced by American Playhouse as a TV featurette.

Keen to explore and develop his style as a filmmaker and pay less attention to the narrative, fictive demands of the feature format, the shorts accorded him a creative liberty, albeit with the relative safety net of his increasing entourage of cast and technical crew. As Hartley wrote in his introduction to the *Surviving Desire* script, 'shorter films can achieve a fullness of expression and execution, while still being essentially sketchy. I appreciate that immediacy. Shorter films don't insist on resolving.' (6)

There are key defining characteristics that are worth cataloguing here. In terms of characters, the films deal in relatively new, though similarly dysfunctional Hartley archetypes: 'young, middle class, college educated, unskilled, white, drunk' (as *Theory Of Achievement* succinctly describes them) whilst the environs of suburban Long Island are substituted, at least in the first two films, for the more urban streets of SoHo and Brooklyn. Collectively, the films focus on the gulf between work and artistic and intellectual ambition and moreover, the division between ideals and reality. In the shorts, as with the features, music is often used to counterpoint and give ironic commentary to an emotional or physical action, with a slap or a lingering kiss being accompanied by a sustained guitar twang. The experimental nature of the films and their mingling of the cerebral with the grittier mechanics of existence (the need to hold down a steady job, the illusory nature of relationships, lack of self-worth) is tempered by Hartley's characteristically aphoristic dialogue: 'we'll get jobs and pay the rent and then get credit cards and be happy,' and slightly off-kilter juxtaposition of the ordinary and the remarkable.

It should be pointed out that *Ambition* and *Theory Of Achievement* are highly rated by Hartley for striking the 'right balance between the pleasures, the plastics of the medium and the pleasures of telling the story.' (7) The director catalogues *Surviving Desire* amongst his lesser works.

Theory Of Achievement (1991)

Cast: Bob Gosse, Jessica Sager, Jeffrey Howard, Elina Löwensohn, Bill Sage, Naledi Tshazibane, M.C. Bailey.

Crew: Direction Hal Hartley, Screenplay Hal Hartley, Cinematography Michael Spiller, Production Design Steven Rosenzweig, Music Jeffrey Howard, Ned Rifle, John Stearns, Editor Hal Hartley, 17.45 minutes.

Story: Downtown Brooklyn, a group of would-be artists and intellectuals, led by a wannabe Real Estate prospector who believes that Brooklyn will, like the Paris of the twenties, become the center of the art world ('but a place people can afford to live') endlessly weigh up the conflicts between paying the rent and pursuing their intellectual ambitions. Unified in inner turmoil and the need for a place to live, the Brooklynites, ultimately take solace from an accordion-led ditty about winning the lottery (a song composed for the film by the actor Jeffrey Howard).

Style: A largely apartment bound short, which could be said to replicate the relative inertia experienced by the characters in the film, *Theory Of Achievement* is visually most notable for Hartley's precision in terms of framing and composition. Cut to the lean, there is nothing extraneous here but that doesn't mean that there is not also room for beauty: a seated Elina Löwensohn bathed in sunlight, a terminally agitated Bill Sage shot from above as he reclines upon a kitchen floor. Shot in bold primary colours, the gentle *ennui* is undercut with typically astute dialogue ('you do what you need to survive and then you are what you become') and a customary humour – such as the rigorous accordion song about the desire to win the lottery (maximum gain with minimum effort) – which warns against taking the philosophical meanderings too seriously.

Subtext: A slightly whimsical riff on the subject of achievement, the short also looks at the creeping inertia that has afflicted an entire generation of artistically aspirant but practically redundant middle-class college leavers keen to create their own cultural nirvana in Brooklyn. Blocking the path to fulfillment is the need to maintain an economic equilibrium (i.e. pay the rent) and the attendant tyranny of work.

Verdict: Intended in part as a portrait of a bunch of Hartley's friends, *Theory Of Achievement* is an affectionate, confidant work. The satirical send-up of artistic wannabe types is countered by the genuine care afforded the characters and the sense of community and camaraderie the film engenders. For anyone whose life has yet to reach the glittering heights promised by a college education, the film is essential viewing.

Ambition (1991)

Cast: George Feaster, Patricia Sullivan, Rick Groel, Jim McCauley, David Troup, Bob Gosse, Bill Sage.

Crew: Direction Hal Hartley, Screenplay Hal Hartley, Cinematography Michael Spiller, Production Design Steven Rosenzweig, Music Ned Rifle, Editor Hal Hartley, 9 minutes.

Story: 'I'm good at what I do,' constantly declares a confident New Yorker whose journey to earn his daily bread is punctuated by armed street assailants, all of whom the man ultimately defeats. At work, the man basks in the admiration and awe of his mostly female colleagues before succumbing to a silent interrogation by his superiors who attempt to undermine his sense of self worth and imperative ideals. More violence ensues.

Style: Set partly in an art gallery, the film's strong compositional sense is accentuated by the striking reds and blues that define the film. Hartley contrasts sound and image to inventive effect, most specifically when a boss vehemently interrogates the protagonist with questions we never hear. Similarly, in one of the final set pieces (which seems to, in advance of *Amateur* pastiche action sequences and reveal Hartley's interest in slapstick), a female voice-over repeats mantras such as 'your ambitions come to nothing,' also revealing the director's aptness to 'loop' and repeat elements of his dialogue.

Subtext: 'No matter what I achieve I always have this irritating sensation of emptiness and futility.' If it can be said to be truly about anything at all, then *Ambition* can perhaps best be identified as being a playful vignette about how our ambitions and ideals are sabotaged by the jobs we have to do and the indignities we have to suffer in order to earn a crust. The continued interest in staccato bursts of violence, here depicted with set pieces that operate as perfectly choreographed, mini-ballets (the film resembles a performance piece by DV8), and personal attack is also extended to signify a refusal to deny the import of culture: 'I love France because of Victor Hugo.'

Verdict: Considered to be Hartley's most Godardian work, though *Theory Of Achievement* most overtly and playfully references Godard with its look-alike character dispensing cultural enlightenment; the film is deliberately oblique and undeniably adventurous, ultimately revealing a director willing to embrace and have fun with the medium.

Surviving Desire (1991)

Cast: Martin Donovan (Jude), Mary Ward (Sofie), Matt Malloy (Henry), Rebecca Nelson (Katie), Julie Sukman (Jill).

Crew: Direction Hal Hartley, Screenplay Hal Hartley, Cinematography Michael Spiller, Production Design Steven Rosenzweig, Music Ned Rifle, The Great Outdoors, Editor Hal Hartley, 60 minutes.

Story: Jude, a Dostoevsky fixated but apathetic literature professor doubting of his ability to impart knowledge to his impatient class falls helplessly in love with Sophie, one of his more tolerant students. Despite the misgivings of confidante Henry, a mature student with a fear of the world ('I've been in school all my life, I don't know how to do anything'), Jude embarks upon a torrid affair. Sophie however soon extinguishes his romantic illusions, revealing herself as not afraid of exploiting her own beauty to get what she wants. Before dismissing his class, the crest-fallen Jude finally consents to teach them something, writing the epigrammatic 'knowing is not enough' on the blackboard as he regales them with biographical details of the Russian author's life.

Style: Ostensibly more traditional in narrative terms, the film deviates in two essential sequences that reveal Hartley's sense of daring and refusal to obey a strict adherence to naturalism or genre. Elated by a kiss, Jude and two passers-by create a wonderfully choreographed dance sequence straight out of *West Side Story* (with deliberate references to Madonna and the crucifixion). If this sequence, later approximated in *Simple Men*, shows the director indulging his escapist tendencies (though Hartley himself feels that the sequence in its totality is ultimately a 'complex expression of vague doom' (8)), another draws attention to the mechanics of the medium and the relationship between sound and image. A band performs a love song in the street as Jude, a charismatic performance from Martin Donovan who radiates his customary, oft-vented frustration in a series of slaps and punches, and Henry go about their business unawares. Other onlookers celebrate the impromptu moment by dancing with abandonment. The film's sense of framing and composition is as astute as ever (the final shot of Jude in the gutter was powerful enough for the director to repeat it in *Amateur*), as is the witty and penetrating dialogue in which characters unburden themselves of their innermost thoughts whilst revealing the clichés of romantic discourse: 'if you never see me again will you carry your disappointment around with you forever?'

Subtext: Heavy with literary references: the title character (Jude The obscure, obvious but cute), the fact that two of the central characters work in a bookstore, the endlessly taught sequence from *The Brothers Karamazov* ('it's an important paragraph,' deadpans Jude), *Surviving Desire* has been described by the director as 'a celebration of a man's capacity for self-destruction. Or, to go easier on our protagonist, the story of a man who disregards the knowledge he possesses in favour of something he finds he cannot possess.' (9) Written over a month long period, Hartley had been inspired by the 'knowing is not enough' quote after it had been sent to him in a Christmas card. Less a love story than a story of love in bad faith, the film nonetheless deals with the euphoria and turmoil of the most precarious of emotions. As well as the general interest in culture and the attainment of knowledge, *Surviving Desire* looks at the disposability of popular culture ('I love that song but hate the video'), faith, the ways in which relationships, often dysfunctional, exist on terms relating to bartering and negotiation (reminiscent of *The Unbelievable Truth* and *Trust*) and the inability to take one's place in the real world. As Jude says to Henry, 'you don't live in the real world, you live in books and ideals.' The film also looks forward to *Flirt* in its assertion that 'perhaps it's not as important to know the answers as it is to ask the questions better.'

Verdict: Offering a distillation of what are commonly seen as Hartley's preoccupations and attributes, the film is largely revered by fans of the director's formally less adventurous but endearingly romantic earlier work. That's not to say that the earlier films do not deal with serious social issues and here a seemingly certifiable, homeless woman who attempts to shanghai passers-by into marriage injects a harsher tone. Hartley never takes things too seriously however, as when Jude discloses that he has penned a beautiful poem, only to spill beer all over it, and in the final analysis, hermetic as it is, *Surviving Desire* is an assiduously charming work.

Simple Men (1992)

Cast: Robert Burke (Bill McCabe), Bill Sage (Dennis McCabe), Karen Sillas (Kate), Elina Löwensohn (Elina), Martin Donovan (Martin), M.C Bailey (Mike), Christopher Cooke (Vic), Jeffrey Howard (Ned Rifle), Damian Young (Sheriff), John MacKay (William McCabe).

Crew: Direction Hal Hartley, Screenplay Hal Hartley, Cinematography Michael Spiller, Production Design Daniel Ouellette, Music Ned Rifle, Editing Steve Hamilton, 104 minutes.

Story: In the throes of an armed computer robbery, career criminal Bill McCabe is double-crossed by his girlfriend when she flees with his partner. Meanwhile, Bill's brother Dennis, a promising if overly serious philosophy student has become obsessed with tracking down their father, a recently escaped former Brooklyn Dodgers baseball shortstop turned radical political activist wanted for his supposed part in a bomb attack on the pentagon. The brothers visit their mother who is readying to flee the family coop for Florida, sending her off significantly richer when Bill gifts her his share of the heist and Dennis bestows her his scholarship fees.

Now a fugitive from the law, Bill needs to get out of town and so accompanies his impoverished brother to Lindenhurst, a Long Island suburb that is as far their meager funds take them. An embittered Bill swears an oath of vengeance on womankind for his broken heart but finds his plans to 'fuck' the first beautiful blond woman he sees interrupted by a brush with the local law. Together the brothers are forced to hastily flee on a motorbike Bill has acquired.

En route to an address where Dennis believes William McCabe may be holding out, they encounter Kate, a recently divorced restaurant owner and her enigmatic, epileptic friend Elina, who seems to be connected with William McCabe in some unspecified way. In fear of her psychotic ex-husband, Kate asks the pair to stay and Bill finds himself putting his plans for revenge on hold as he hopelessly falls for her, much to the chagrin of a local fisherman, Martin.

Meanwhile, when Dennis – who has inadvertently alerted the lovelorn sheriff of his and Bill's presence – has his affections for Elina spurned, he correctly concludes that she is his father's mistress and conspires to allow her to lead him to William McCabe. The anarchist patriarch is awaiting escape on the boat owned by Martin and Dennis confronts him with his crimes. Convinced of his innocence, Dennis makes arrangements for brother Bill to also flee justice across the ocean.

Having decided upon a life of domestic bliss, Bill is loath to leave but is offered little alternative when Kate refuses to corroborate the alibi that would disconnect him from his computer crime. After speeding to the quayside to join his father, Bill suffers a change of heart and decides to return to Kate to pledge his commitment to her. Shrugging off the attentions of the awaiting law, Bill and Kate are briefly reunited.

Background: The central premise actually came to Hartley long before he had established himself as a director. The idea of two very different brothers searching for their lost father was gradually honed with the addition of the device of having the father appear as a former sports star who had turned to radical political activism in the 1960's. Another addition was the character Elina, an epileptic Romanian radical, introduced after Hartley had been transfixed by working with Elina Löwensohn on *Theory Of Achievement* and determined to write her a larger part.

Again teaming up with British production outfit Zenith, Film Four International and American Playhouse, Hartley also found himself working with new production and financing parties. Fine Line Features, the boutique arm of mini-studio New Line came on board, as did BIM Distribuzione. Having garnered critical approbation and built up a committed arthouse following both in the U.S and in Europe, the reward was a significant increase in budget. Made for $2 million, *Simple Men* is considered the last of Hartley's Long Island pictures though it was for the most part actually shot in Houston, Texas. So how did Hartley make Texas look like a Long Island suburb? 'It was very easy...we avoided photographing indigenous vegetation. And whatever was red, we painted white. We put fish up everywhere.' (10) Keen to move away from shooting close to home, the director did however make Long Island an integral part of the film, actually taking the topography into question with the oceanic escape at the end of the picture.

As evidence of Hartley's increasing stature, *Simple Men* was selected for Official Competition at the 1992 Cannes Film Festival.

Style: Stylistically more audacious perhaps than *Trust*, *Simple Men* certainly continues the director's favouring of ellipticism over convention, specifically in its challenging, invigorating but nonetheless playful toying with narrative arcs and its omission of establishing shots; a technique that makes the material feel fresh and immediate. Beginning on black in mid-robbery, the words 'don't move' are uttered to a blindfolded security guard who when asked if he moved concurs that he may have done because his foot has gone to sleep. It is at this early stage also worth noting that the film elliptically ends as it begins but this time with Bill being told not to move and in a vulnerable position. The ending again shows Hartley striving for honesty and refusing to grant his protagonists' complete closure or happiness. Interestingly, the film originally ended with the sheriff demanding, 'Kate, do you know this man?' to which Kate replied, 'Yes, I know this man.' Uneasy with the conclusion, Hartley instead went with an alternative, a variation on the ending of *Trust*, claiming that 'it feels right. It seems necessary. Unavoidable, even.' (11) Hartley's original intention became the ending of *Amateur*.

Whilst the guard's dialogue and the scene in general plays with the established customs associated with the heist genre, it also throws the disorientated spectator immediately off-guard (the framing of the characters too is decidedly off kilter), snaring the viewer's attention. Likewise, later on there is a fade to black on the brothers and the film opens again without explanation on an intense conversation between Karen and Elina. The conversation is unconnected to anything that has gone before, is between two characters of which we have no prior knowledge and is an entirely different locale; a very picturesque, rural (a first for Hartley) one as it happens. It's as if Hartley is demanding the undivided attention of those who are watching.

This technique will be clear to those who have followed his work and in other ways too Hartley adds elements that suggest that *Simple Men* is part of a work in progress, referencing out to motifs, touches and occurrences recognisable from his past endeavors. There's the continued reference to Ned Rifle (a troubled character, smitten by the air of adventure he believes Bill to inhabit), the respect for people who fix things (the opposing characters of the brothers continues the director's culture versus class dichotomy) and the continued slapping, punching and shoving between characters (as well as the regular slaps for indiscretions and examples of machismo, a nun and a cop brawl unceremoniously in the street). There's also the act of having characters read aloud from books (William McCabe quotes to a selected audience from a book titled *Anarchy*) and the hide-and-seek sequence that seems to be freely borrowed from a *Restoration* farce. In this instance Dennis is led a merry dance around Kate's house by Elina. The intricately constructed dialogue again has an intentional air of circularity and repetiveness about it, as evidenced in the conversation between Bill and Dennis about having a broken heart and more effectively perhaps in the scene where a drunken Bill and Martin talk about getting emotional when drunk. The conversation begins at one point, moves on to somewhere else and returns to its original point before, like a dog chasing its tail, skirting around in circles.

Mike's hilarious electric guitar rendition of *Greensleeves* also marks a return to the fondness for filming people playing music as exhibited in *The Unbelievable Truth* and *Surviving Desire*. Moreover, the continually sparring Mike and Vic appear as the same characters they played in the director's debut; Vic is freshly divorced and terminally cantankerous whilst Mike, in a moment typical of the film's rich, often absurd humour (the foibles of men and small ironies are a regular Hartley preoccupation), spends his time learning French in order to pick up a woman, who it transpires is Italian. An attempt to 'elicit this feeling of a curiously small world' (12), this piece of intertextuality was inspired by Hartley's watching Lindsay Anderson's *O Lucky Man!*

Still often choosing to use tableaux set-ups, *Simple Men* also develops Hartley's interest in 'conveying a sense of the landscape graphically, in juxtaposition to the human form.' (13) Hartley and Spiller, filming in bold colours, in the first part of the film at least and more autumnal, subdued ones for the scenes at Kate's, again imbue almost every shot with increased signification, capturing figures at crossroads, in front of STOP signs and generally in interesting contrast to their surroundings. There is also, in part a result of the bigger budget, an increased assurance in terms of the look of the film and a more expansive use of camera movement. The brothers speeding away from Ned Rifle on the bike is comparatively edge-of-the-seat stuff in consideration of the static camera Hartley had previously favoured/been forced to use for economic reasons. Likewise, there's an increased use of tracking and panning shots, not least in the scene where the camera pans in on Kate on her stoop at the end of the movie.

Peppered with poignancy and a trademark philosophical inquisitiveness, Hartley's droll, perceptive dialogue (Ned's 'there's nothing like a machine to make a man feel insignificant' is one of many stand-out lines) also stops to mediate on popular culture in a scene which discusses Madonna and whether she is exploiting her own talent – exploitation being one of the key themes of the film – or merely herself being exploited. It's an important moment that stops to very carefully consider how popular culture and iconic female figures inform our perceptions of femininity but it's gently underscored by Martin's apparent confusion and wish to simply compile a list of his favourite rock-bands.

Abundant in small epiphanies such as Bill's wish to act 'thoughtful, deep, modest and possibly dangerous' only to be perceived of as being so when he is at his most natural, there is also a favouring of often highly appropriate, organising epigrammatic statements or slogans, such as the 'there's only trouble and desire' piece of advice delivered by Bill that punctures Ned's dream of the world as being a place of 'adventure and romance.' These adages are in keeping with the overall style of the film and Hartley's wish to communicate thought and meaning with precision and a minimum of fuss.

Subtext: Already tentatively discussed is one of the overriding themes of the film, that of questions of exploitation and objectification regarding women. This theme extends to what is undoubtedly another primary concerns, the way that men look at women, their changing attitudes towards them and how men often seek to reconcile their needs in them. Bill's brooding misogyny is manifest in his detailed speech to brother Dennis about finding a pretty, blond woman he can use up, treat like trash and then throwaway but ultimately of course Bill amends his attitude, learning through the already wronged Kate – whose track record she attests extends to psychopaths and liars – the values of commitment and respect. If Bill starts out constantly thinking with his dick, Dennis seems to take an almost asexual attitude towards women (displayed in the scene where he innocently fishes for a note from between the legs of an adolescent schoolgirl) until he develops a strong attraction for his father's mistress. Claiming that he has no respect for his father but that he respects his father's taste in women, to which Elina – alongside Kate another of Hartley's independent, intelligently drawn female characters – replies 'then go make love with your mother,' Dennis' attitude towards women seems to be inspired by his protective relationship with his mother. Both Bill and Dennis are shown to defer to her and treat her with the utmost respect with Dennis' desire to track down his father shown to be more of a result of William McCabe's womanising and breaking up of the family than for his radical politics. There is then an overt Oedipal subtext to the film, comically flagged when Bill cries out that he has been betrayed by the woman he loves and Dennis replies, 'Who? Mom?'

From the McCabe's to Vic to Kate, it is also worth noting that the film is again littered with dysfunctional families and frustrated people in unsatisfactory relationships. Perhaps suffering the most is the disconsolate sheriff, wonderfully played by Damian Young, whose uneasy time at home leads him to proclaim that 'love is a myth invented in a torture chamber in hell' and to passionately ask 'why do women exist?' The sheriff is another prime example of Hartley constantly undermining audience expectations. The pillar of community, there to offer security, promise and trust, the sheriff is a physical wreck, unable to get through a confrontation without a reassuring

41

pat on the back. Likewise, the 'dangerous, psychotic, angry Jack' turns out, after Hartley has cranked up the tension with angled shots of a red sports car, to be a rather meek fellow who has returned to Kate's because he is cold and in need of a jacket. The characters Hartley creates simply refuse to conform to stereotypes (a nun who smokes and brawls in the street!) and there's a marked gender reversal in that the men – Hartley again gently mocks the male species throughout – are confused and emotionally inadequate whilst the women are forthright and know exactly what they want.

When making the film Hartley believed it to be significantly removed from his other works, specifically in terms of subject matter but has since accepted that it shares a very consistent world outlook that can be condensed to the fact that 'you don't get something for nothing, ever.' (14) Beyond this outlook, *Simple Men* has clear thematic associations with Hartley's previous work in other key regards to those I have already mentioned. There's the passing references to religion (the nun and the Virgin Mary medallion), the respect for practical skills, a 'consequential' (the director's description) interest in politics and political actions, the distrust, suspicion and rumour mongering that is rife in small towns (Dennis' innocent 'I'm not from around here' is what sets in motion the flight from Lindenhurst) and a concern for the environment (Kate plants trees because they are good for the ozone). Moreover, there is the feeling throughout of lives tinged with unhappiness and a frustrating sense of incompleteness and it is tempting to suggest that without the director's deft touch, gift for irony and comic sensibilities, the film's could make for dour, almost unremittingly morose viewing.

Key Moment: Screeching to a halt in his truck, the pent-up Martin jumps from the driver's seat and screams, 'I can't stand the quiet!' The film cuts to Kate's bar and the sound of Sonic Youth. Elina leads Dennis, Martin and finally Bill and Kate through a hypnotic, elaborately choreographed dance routine in which the performers shake their stuff in tandem to both each other and the high-volume music.

The musical interlude is a moment of wonderful abandonment that successfully develops Hartley's interest in musical pieces (music, movement and dance recurring throughout his work), previously perhaps most clearly evidenced in *Surviving Desire*. Geoff Andrew points out in his authoritative book on maverick American directors, *Stranger Than Paradise*, that the sequence has import regarding the development of the film in that it suggests the ever-shifting allegiances and suspicions of the dancers through their subtle glances and gestures but it can also be enjoyed as an inspired and exhilarating juncture on a purely sensory level.

Comparisons with Godard in terms of form and the approach to constructing meaning often flow thick and fast in connection to Hartley's work and there's little doubting that the moment seems to have been influenced by the beguiling, impromptu dance sequence in *Bande à Part*. It does however again conclusively conclude that Hartley is no chilly formalist and that he imbues his work with a mischievous and endearing sense of fun.

Music: Composing using the alias Ned Rifle, Hartley delivers a winning, relatively low-key, guitar-synthesizer driven score. The end credit sequence composition is especially affecting and captures the gently melancholic, wistful tone of the film.

There's a characteristic and plentiful infusion of powerful U.S rock on the soundtrack too with perennial favourites such as Sonic Youth and Yo La Tengo – whose *Always Something* is particularly good – all putting in audio appearances.

Verdict: Without diluting his ideas or sacrificing his principles, *Simple Men* sees Hartley negotiating the larger budget with aplomb. More attractively packaged perhaps than previous features – the use of new locations certainly feels like a breath of fresh air and the higher production values are another beneficiary of the extra financial injection – it's still recognisably a Hal Hartley picture and is marked by its director's customary invention, rigour and wit. Again refusing to ally itself to any one specific genre, though there are clearly elements of the road movie, the film marks a sense of progression in the wider context of Hartley's career. There's a wider range of characters (all wonderfully brought to life by the regular cast), digressive plot strands and a heightened interplay between the director and his audience. Importantly, Hartley displays a mindfulness of the need to engage with issues of concern without didacticism, creating a film that appeals to both the head and the heart. 4/5.

Recent Shorts

As Hartley's career has progressed and naturally evolved he has continued to use the short format as an arena in which he can expand his visions, confound the expectations of audiences and 'fans' and inquisitively explore experimental techniques and approaches to production. 'I always feel more playful with the shorter films. It makes me think that one can be serious without being deep. Intelligent without being heavy.' (15)

The continuing ardors of obtaining funding for feature production and the innovations in and practicalities of digital technology, a technology Hartley has mastered despite his preference for the more mechanical, tactile elements of the medium, have also helped facilitate his increasing enthusiasm for working in a field that does not necessitate extensive crews, budgets or a commitment to convention.

In terms of a prevalent artistic sensibility or aesthetic, Hartley's recent shorts have tended to 'evolve out of the collision of qualities in perhaps disparate images and sounds' (16) and the desire to look and juxtapose both sound and image without preconception. The director has talked of a desire to make films that can be appreciated in a similar manner to a piece of music or a painting, open to endless and instant repetition and interpretation. Unburdened by the fear of failure or expectation but ever respectful of some of the basic constituents of filmmaking (story, character and dialogue) Hartley has residually allowed his more esoteric, experimental shorts to influence and complement his features and indeed vice versa.

Iris (1993)

Cast: Parker Posey, Sabrina Lloyd. 3:50 minutes.

Comment: Produced as part of the *Red Hot No Alternative* series, *Iris* incorporates the track of the same name by The Breeders to produce a complex, symbolically charged short film/ pop promo. Filmed in trademark bold colours, the piece ably demonstrates the director's acute spatial awareness and various shots, such as an aerial view of one of the characters gripping weights, echo the idiosyncratic approach to the positioning of figures and objects within the frame. Also evident, is Hartley's Bressonian tendencies (as is his art background; classical paintings serve as a backdrop for two scenes) and his concentration upon a small gesture or intricately produced detail: for instance a porcelain white hand brushing across a crimson dress.

Iris is also reflective of Hartley's work in pop promos and has its leads repeating the lyrics of the pop record as if an incantation. Similarly, there's a marked experimental approach to the use of sound with the spectator subjected to a soundtrack of dripping water (something of a motif in Hartley's shorter pieces), twittering birds and brief audio bursts of the actual song which acts as a very loose framework for the film. A dense work that is difficult to unravel, what is clear is that the piece acts as a characteristically witty treatise on exorbitant property prices and the strain of making economical ends meet as the women openly discuss mortgage percent rates and bemoan the fact that 'owning is bondage.' Karl Marx would approve. *Iris* also carries connotations regarding the representation of women, its final shot being the image of the set of weights finally being lifted.

NYC 3/94 (1994)

Cast: Dwight Ewell, Liana Pai, Paul Schultze, James Urbaniak.

Crew: Direction Hal Hartley, Screenplay Hal Hartley, Camera/Monitor Assistant M.C Bailey, Sound Jeanne Gilliland, 9 minutes.

Comment: The film intercuts between three characters (Ewell, Pai and Schultze) caught up in a series of ground and aerial attacks on New York in March 1994. Meanwhile, a studio bound man (Urbaniak), offers an analysis of events to a microphone. Characteristically vivid in its use of colour and compositional style, *NYC 3/94* is perhaps most notable for its juxtaposition of sound and image which features a constant audio barrage of helicopters, angry crowd noise and machine-gun bursts to economically denote the off-screen mayhem and duress. The piece continues Hartley's interest in dance and movement, most specifically in a scene that has the three principal characters veering dramatically down an empty New York thoroughfare. Highly ambiguous, *NYC 3/94* perhaps on the most simplistic of levels offers an observation on the rigors of modern urban living but there's also an underlying political stance to the film, with Urbaniak's commentator quoting from various texts on the subject of rights and asserting 'it must be difficult to represent a gruesome aspect of reality without making it political.'

Structurally complex work but improving with repeated viewings, *NYC 3/94* is audacious and daring enough to provoke no end of intellectual inquiry. Produced as part of the *NYC Postcards* series, the film has taken on a telling resonance since the terrorist attacks on New York of September 11th 2001 and invites parallels with the attacks on New York depicted in *No Such Thing*.

Opera No.1 (1994)

Cast: Patricia Dunnock (Woman), Parker Posey (Fairy 1) Adrienne Shelly (Fairy 2), James Urbaniak (Man).

Crew: Direction Hal Hartley, Screenplay, Hal Hartley, Cinematography Michael Spiller, Production Design Steve Rosenzweig, Music Hal Hartley, Editor Steve Silkensen, 8 minutes.

Comment: The fact that Hartley had long since incorporated elements from various musical genres in his work (the Hollywood musical, angst-ridden rock performances, the Hollywood musical via the French New Wave), his increasing interest in classical and classical modes of music and his appetite for disparate types of performance art ensured that it came as little surprise when he announced plans to write, score and direct a mini-opera. Or, as the opening titles of Opera No. 1 has it, 'a small film (with music).'

Impressively staged in what appears to be a derelict warehouse, the visually sumptuous *Opera No. 1* concerns the attempts of two rollerblading, bohemian fairies (including Shelly, Hartley's former muse working with the director for the first time in years) to instigate a romantic affair between a lovelorn woman and her bookish male counterpart. Trouble is, both mortals seem more interested in a romantic liaison with the matchmaker. The film returns to familiar thematic terrain in its consideration of loneliness, the barriers intellect can erect to the path of emotional fulfillment ('why do smart men forget everything they know when a girl smiles at them') and the sheer complicatedness of relationships. The film also retains a keen interest in physical slapstick, with an eye on the importance of gesture in Opera, with the mortal man and woman grappling and banging each other's heads against a wall before being finally forced to romantically interact.

A warm and witty work that that contains such comic interplay as: 'you're perfect,' 'well I am immortal,' *Opera No. 1* has fun with the structure of the milieu in which the director is operating, even including a short intermission with overdubbed applause.

The Other Also (1997)

Cast: Miho Nikaido, Elina Löwensohn and the voice of James Urbaniak.
Crew: Uncredited. Running time 11 minutes approx.
Comment: Commissioned by *The Foundation Cartier* for a show in Paris titled *Amour, The Other Also* is a hypnotic, initially impenetrable performance piece that is reflective of the director's assertion that as a filmmaker

he continually thinks primarily in terms of movement. 'When I isolate the primary elements of film I find photography, movement and sound recording – in that order.' (17)

Shot on Digital Video in one afternoon with the assistance of a small crew of students, the piece features the blurred, shimmering figures of Miho Nikaido and Elina Löwensohn who slowly rotate within the frame, passing in front of and across one another's path. The relationship between sound and image is examined, with the images being accompanied by an audio track that features dripping tap, a mournful, elegiac synthesized score and the voice of Urbaniak intoning, 'I say unto you, do not resist anyone. If anyone strikes you on the right cheek then turn to him the other also.'

Extremely subliminal in tone and structure, the words do however carry overt religious connotations, religion and faith being a defining theme in Hartley's work and indeed background. The presence of Hartley alumni in even his most challenging forays suggests the trust, confidence and inspiration he inspires amongst both cast and crew.

The New Math(s) (2000)

Cast: DJ Mendel, David Neumann, Miho Nikaido.

Crew: Direction Hal Hartley, Screenplay Hal Hartley, Cinematography Richard Sylvarnes, Choreography DJ Mendel, Music Louis Andriessen and Michael Van Der AA, Editor Ben Tudhope, 15 minutes.

Comment: A True Fiction Pictures production in conjunction with the BBC, *The New Maths(s)* was part of series of short pieces titled *Sound On Film* collectively commissioned to look at how various contemporary film directors and composers conspire to explore that very subject. Also including collaborations between Nicolas Roeg/ Adrian Utley and Werner Herzog/John Tavener, the films received their world premiere at the Barbican Centre on March 1st 2001.

Hal Hartley's entry to the series certainly encapsulates his desire to approach film as if it were a piece of music whilst also fully embodying his thinking of film primarily in terms of movement. Close in spirit to *The Other Also*, the film retains many of the visual pleasures commonly associated with Hartley's best work. Like *Opera No.1* the piece boasts imaginative use of interiors, taking part in an industrial building that houses pistachio coloured cogs and wheels and is beautifully lit by Frank Stubblefield. Sylvarnes' camerawork is inventive and fresh, often shooting the three principals (one of which is an uptight, permanently pacing teacher with a resemblance to big-collared comedian Harry Hill) from oblique angles and commonly from way down low, most effectively perhaps in the scenes in which we see them riding a battered warehouse lift.

Wildly open to interpretation, *The New Math(s)* seems on the most basic of levels to look at forms of knowledge (like *Surviving Desire* there is also an examination of teacher/pupil relations), power shifts between male and female (with a nod to the mythology of Adam and Eve as denoted by the symbolism of the red apple) and the director's continuing fascination with the precision of machinery, a precision replicated in the highly choreographed movements of the performers. In this regard Hartley benefits immeasurably from Nuemann's expertise with the often intricate and complex physical sequences achieving a sustained brio and effect. Moreover, Nuemann's choreography seems to consciously play upon some of the physical motifs we have come to expect from Hartley's work and there are numerous slaps, punches and engagements in combat (often accompanied by martial arts sound effects on the soundtrack) to be enjoyed.

The audio track is indeed meticulously detailed throughout, utilising 'found' sounds (tapping, industrial noise and bleeps) to inventive and provocative effect. The specially composed score by Andriessen and Van Der AA incorporates, as is often Hartley's wont when composing, elements from jazz, rock, classical and opera.

On the whole, the piece feels more confident, playful (there's a neat sight gag that involves the so-called math(s) experts adding on their fingers) and somewhat 'looser' than Hartley's previous attempts to incorporate the sometimes homogeneous, sometimes discordant mediums of film, music, dance and theatre.

Kimono (2000)

A cyclical piece about a bride (Miho Nikaido), dumped from a car who finds her way back to the beginning of the story, I originally saw the film in a late night slot on television but unable to obtain a copy to elucidate further, I make only a passing reference to it here.

Amateur (1994)

Cast: Isabelle Huppert (Isabelle), Martin Donovan (Thomas), Elina Löwensohn (Sofia), Damian Young (Edward), Chuck Montgomery (Jan), David Simonds (Kurt), Pamela Stewart (Officer Melville)

Crew: Direction Hal Hartley, Screenplay Hal Hartley, Cinematography Michael Spiller, Production Design, Steve Rosenzweig, Music Jeffrey Taylor and Ned Rifle, Editing Steve Hamilton, 100 minutes.

Story: A man, Thomas, lays unconscious in a cobbled New York street. A woman, Sofia, inspects his body then flees, believing him to be dead.

Thomas revives and though badly hurt staggers to a nearby diner. Flinging his Dutch change onto the counter, Thomas has no idea who he is as his injury has led to severe amnesia. Isabelle, a former nun now trying – and failing – to make a career writing pornography takes pity on Thomas and invites him back to her apartment. Isabelle asks Thomas to make love to her, claiming that she is a nymphomaniac who has never had sex because she is 'choosy.' Sadly, Thomas is too tired.

Sofia meanwhile contacts Edward, an accountant who once worked with Thomas at a multinational corporation that produced pornographic films and reveals to him that she has killed Thomas, her violent, abusive pornographer husband. It was whilst working for this organisation that Thomas forced Sofia into working in porno films. Edward warns Sofia to keep a low profile on account of the fact Thomas was attempting to bribe the head of the corporation, Jacques, with some computer discs containing details of Jacques involvement in arms deals. Wanting to start a new life and become 'a mover and a shaker', Sofia rekindles the blackmail threats with disastrous consequences; all set to join Sofia at a swank Porchester residence belonging to a client, Edward is kidnapped from Grand Central Station by Jan and Kurt, two thugs sent by Jacques to ascertain Sofia's whereabouts. Edward is brutally tortured.

Having briefly met in a local cinema, Isabelle recognises Sofia as the infamous porn star Sofia Ludens and connects the seemingly gentle Thomas with her after he threateningly mentions her in his sleep. Convinced that she has found a purpose to her life, Isabelle forces Thomas to go back to his apartment to pick up the threads of his past life. Isabelle sheds her conservative garb and dresses in a sexy black leather outfit belonging to Sofia, who also returns to the apartment trailed by Kurt and Jan who capture her and set to work with a pair of pliers. When Jan exits to check the computer discs he finds on Sofia, Thomas and Isabelle save Sofia, whom Thomas does not recognise, killing Kurt by forcing him out of a window. The three of them escape to the Porchester house, with Jan close in tow. En route, Sofia refuses to talk to Thomas or reveal his past.

Edward, still suffering the after-effects of his ordeal, is arrested for disturbing the peace and hauled off to the police station. The attempts of the kindly Officer Melville to help him backfire when Edward recognises a photo of Thomas and uses Melville's gun to shoot his way out of the station to head to Porchester. Edward arrives at the house in time to slay Jan but Sofia is also injured in the shoot-out. Isabelle takes her to her former convent for treatment and whilst recovering Sofia finally elucidates on Thomas' past. Unaware of his crimes but prepared to apologise for them, Isabelle recognises that Thomas is a changed man and the pair assent to make love. However, when Thomas goes to fetch the car, police sharpshooters are waiting for him. Mistaking him for Edward they shoot him dead.

Background: Whilst touring Europe as part of a publicity campaign for *Simple Men*, Hartley, who has always been a popular figure there, hence the increasing availability of European funds, began to develop a beleaguered sense of alienation. A recuperative trip to Amsterdam provided inspiration – and for the diner scene loose change – for the film's thematic kernel: the wish to escape and flee responsibility.

The notion of responsibility was also uppermost in Hartley's mind due to the pressures of running True Fiction Pictures, which had developed into a sizeable role necessitating more and more time and energy. Hartley's realisation that he did not want to be an accountable businessman not only informed another preoccupation of *Amateur* – the film is riddled with business jargon – but also led to his making Thomas a film producer, albeit of the pornographic variety.

It was another *Simple Men* inspired event that led to Hartley's drawing of the parallel in the film between the business world and the crime world. Basking in the glory of *Simple Men's* Cannes showing, Hartley was introduced to people who detailed how capital from gun-running out of Israel and the Middle East and other illegal activities often wound its way into pornography and film related businesses; 'It was the only time I became interested in crime, and I believe it was by virtue of its resemblance to business-as usual in my own field. The story I ended up writing seemed to function as a neat example of how ferocious crime can trickle down into our more mundane experiences.' (18)

It is also important to consider the circumstances leading to the involvement of Isabelle Huppert, recognised as one of France's greatest actresses after performances in films such as: *La Cérémonie*, *Loulou* and Godard's *Passion*. An admirer of *Trust* and Hartley's ability to write strong, three-dimensional female characters, Huppert contacted the director and suggested that they work together. Partly inspired by Glenda Jackson's maverick nun in Michael Lindsay-Hogg's *Nasty Habits*, and the aforementioned experiences, Hartley set to work on the first draft of the script which initially featured Huppert 'narrating the scenes as if she were the omniscient author.' (19) An attempt to draw attention to the artifice of storytelling, this approach was abandoned for failing to be of sufficient interest. The director has since admitted that the knowledge of Huppert's involvement created certain pressures during the writing stages, compelling him to come up with something less radical, more linear and certainly more accessible than his earlier works. The result is an idiosyncratic concession to a genre picture, a work described to *Time Out* critic Geoff Andrew as 'an action thriller with one flat tyre.' (20)

Style: The title of the film patently applies to the characters who are forced to tentatively make their way in situations that are new and alien to them; Thomas, Sofia and Isabelle have all left behind worlds they knew well and are now amateurs at the new roles, hence Isabelle's confusing pornography with poetry and Sofia's disastrous attempts at bribery. The title of the film equally refers to Hartley himself, making his first foray into the thriller genre. With the film the director set himself the task of looking at the world afresh and he envisioned using characters that were uninformed as a means of achieving this aim.

Hartley's previous work, though working to defy easy categorisation, can be allied with the melodrama; *Amateur* is a tragedy. We are used to seeing a lack of resolution at the end of Hartley's films and the denial of complete closure, romantic or otherwise. However, though Hartley's male protagonists may suffer a rebuke and be forced to face up to imprisonment, *Amateur* concludes with a noticeably changed Thomas forced to pay the highest price not only for his previous indiscretions but, in a case of mistaken identity, for the actions of Edward.

The director himself views the film as 'standard TV cop show stuff, but with the information changed. A TV cop show made by someone who doesn't know how to make TV cop shows.' (21) How then does the director set about changing this information and bring his own Hartleyesque stamp to the outwardly dark proceedings? There's the usual absurdity and creation of eccentric characters and situations. Where else would you find a character that is an ex-nun who also happens to be a nymphomaniac who hasn't actually ever had sex? In fact many of the characters are variations on recognisable types, imbued with their own individual quirks and unique peculiarities. The ruthless heavies Kurt and Jan may know how to torture someone with a domestic lamp but they are hopelessly inept when it comes to choosing a mobile phone that will give them a reliable reception. Officer Melville is no hard-bitten cop but a softie, apt to burst into tears when confronted with another hard luck story. Hartley's typically wry dialogue is also present and is another means by which he italicizes situations and generic conventions; the all-important floppy discs are, as both Sofia and Thomas point out neither 'floppy nor round.' Throughout the film Hartley seems to offer up situations that are a vital constituent of the milieu in which *Amateur* operates only to then dramatically subvert them. It's a device wholly in keeping with the director's desire to approach filmmaking and narrative conventions from new perspectives and to constantly usurp the expectations of his audience. This element of spectator surprise and the way in which Hartley manipulates what people may expect to see in his films is one of the things that make him so interesting as a filmmaker.

By extension, in earlier chapters I have pointed out the frequently overlooked darker elements at play in the director's work, *Amateur* very self-consciously takes this several steps further. The effects of violence are no longer merely funny; they hurt and have unsettling and often disturbing consequences. Edward's torture is genuinely shocking as are the street scenes immediately after the ordeal. It is in this area too that the language has a harsher edge – the film is obviously thematically concerned with pornography, crime and violence – but Hartley conveys these elements not through graphic depiction but more commonly through what is said and indeed what is left unsaid. For instance, Thomas' capacity for physical violence is revealed when he verbally threatens to take a razor to Sofia's face when sleeping whilst the earthy delights of a Sofia Ludens porno movie are merely whispered into the ear of Thomas by a literature loving schoolboy.

On a formal level, *Amateur* has much in common with Hartley's previous work. There's the continuing disregard for establishing shots (incidentally, the opening image of Donovan in the gutter is a repeat of the closing shot of *Surviving Desire* which the director didn't feel he had got quite right) and indeed for continuity which Hartley claimed 'bugged him' because it got in the way of the image. 'When it came to editing these images I was forced to reconsider the necessity of seamlessness and continuity on a moment-to-moment basis. The way I shot determined that I would have to have ellipses, I would have to have jump cuts.' (22) There is the acute, rigorously precise sense of composition and colour that had become a staple of the director's work, illustrated by the scene in which Isabelle reads her erotic story to her pornographer (a man whose intended career was 'defamatory journalism'). Isabelle is seated on a brightly coloured couch that contrasts sharply with the walls behind her. Also back grounded is a classical painting of a female nude. The moment evokes Hartley's art history grounding plus acts as a reference to Huppert's part in *Passion*. Hartley and Spiller thought long and hard about the shooting of Huppert and were at first in awe of the fact that she represented a significant portion of the history of French cinema. In the end they decided to embrace it, even having the camera duplicate certain movements and gestures from her cinematic past.

The film goes further in replicating iconic images in the freeze frame television picture of Sofia from one of her hardcore videos. The image is based on a photo of Bernini's statue *Ecstasy Of St. Teresa*, and was on the most simplistic of levels (Hartley is expansive on the subject of St. Teresa and her latent sexuality) used to denote Isabelle's recognition of the sign that would spur her into action.

Throughout the film Hartley frequently formally calls into question the relationship between the characters and the confusion and emotional gulf that exists between them. This is done in the first instance in the interesting two shot in the diner Thomas enters where Isabelle is frightening the customers with her bawdy stories. It is later repeated in the shot of Sofia and Thomas in a café en route to Porchester. Seated at separate tables, Sofia is in the foreground and it is on her features and her expressions as Thomas talks that the camera focuses. Hartley has described the scene as the best in the movie in that it sets up a very direct rapport between the spectator and Sofia, a rapport from which Thomas is physically excluded.

Filming on the streets of New York – with much of the filming taking place at night – Hartley attempted to capture what he saw as the physical essence of the city, the reflective surfaces, 'the light in the windows, glass puddles...the kinds of bricks and cobblestones, the architecture, the wash on the buildings on lower Broadway.' (23) As a result, the film has a dark hue, with browns, greens and blues as the dominant colours. Though made on an increased budget, the highest the director has yet had at his disposal, filming in New York did bring certain organisational problems beyond issues such as crowd and noise control. The actual expense was a constant worry, especially to someone renowned for being a stickler for economy, and the production suffered fraught moments during a bout of illness to Martin

Donovan, who was stricken with hepatitis, during re-shoots at the most expensive location, the monastic Cloisters in upper Manhattan. Hartley responded by simply filming the pallid actor often sitting and from behind, considering it a means of positively responding to the circumstances of filmmaking.

Perhaps the final formal feature I wish to detail is the frequent use of expressionistic, geometric angles in the film, not only in the aforementioned physically imposing Cloisters sequence but more interestingly perhaps in the Dockside warehouse location following Edward's torture. The pea-green buildings with their yellow lanterns swaying in the wind are all captured at oblique angles and as Edward stumbles away on the rickety boards using the walls for support, one is reminded of the sets of the expressionistic masterpiece *The Cabinet Of Dr. Caligari*.

Subtext: As revealed, *Amateur* is predominantly concerned with the themes of violence, fear of responsibility, the links between crime and business and pornography. There is also a complicit interest in the ways in which men objectify and treat women purely as sex objects, a recurring theme in Hartley's work. This is suggested early on in Isabelle's date with the creepy Warren in what looks like a porno cinema (memories of *Taxi Driver* abound), where the octopus-armed lothario wastes no time in setting about 'molesting' her. Prior to torturing Sofia, Kurt asks, 'do you resent your position in the motion picture industry? I'm interested in commodities you see and I also find you very attractive,' a moment that acts as a neat adjunct to the conversation regarding issues regarding treating Madonna's body as a commodity in *Simple Men*.

Hartley of course is not adverse to turning the tables and he often reveals the women exploiting their own sexuality to get exactly what they want; Sofia toying with a doorman (played by Michael Imperioli - what is it with Hartley and future *Soprano's* stars?) to gain free entry and Isabelle's shedding off her dowdy frocks to don sexy, leather garb (a reversal of the usual pattern in Hartley's movies). A further spin is added to the issue by the casting of a female (Adria Tennor) as the *Odyssey* loving schoolboy (literature once again appears, books also litter the floor of Isabelle's apartment) with whom Thomas discusses the act of looking at naked pictures of women. Throughout the film the director treads the difficult line between examining objectification and falling foul of it (Kurt's 'wow' on seeing Isabelle armed with phallic drill is a questionable moment) and the film attracted equal praise and damnation from feminists upon its release. The marketing of the film in Europe certainly focused upon the alluring female cast but this is an area over which Hartley has no control and the methodology and intent of the director – who has said that 'if I didn't find people inherently mysterious and intriguing, and by extension sexually appealing, all my characters would be the same' (24) is largely beyond reproach.

There are a fair smattering of other concerns that the director returns to: identity, the search for love, the need for trust and respect in relationships, the role of art and indeed artifice in commonplace, everyday life (more fully developed in *Henry Fool*) and not so thinly veiled references to religion and Hartley's Catholic upbringing. There's also a recurrent political aspect to the film, most overtly in the linkage between crime and business corporations but also in more underplayed, subtle moments such as when Isabelle directs Thomas to the video store, located on the corner 'where the white supremacists hang-out.'

Key Moment: The scene where a deranged Edward repeatedly shoots Jan after arriving at the upstate country house (the sequence, which occurs after some coming and going through doors, thus retaining the element of farce to be often found in Hartley's work) is perhaps the most memorable in the film, both in terms of its execution and how it both relates to and deviates from Hartley's signature representation of violence.

Filmed in a tracking long shot, the sequence has a balletic quality in keeping with Hartley's interest in movement and choreography, with Jan twirling and turning as each bullet hits. This is combined with a slapstick element as Edward frantically flits to and through, adopting various positions from which to offload his bullets. At first the scene, which has a unmistakably surreal quality, appears purely comic – with Edward even disappearing out of shot to charge up a hill before charging back down again to begin re-firing – and entirely in keeping with the often quizzical episodes of violent outbursts that pepper Hartley's work. However, it becomes clear that it serves a more serious purpose.

The highly stylized, determinedly non-naturalistic scene is a refreshing and provocative alternative to conventional shoot-out's and the protocols of the crime/thriller genre. By undermining the expectations of the spectator concerning how such confrontations normally play out in mainstream cinema, Hartley also forces a re-evaluation of anticipation concerning on-screen violence and gunplay. In the build-up to the scene, originally conceived of as a slightly pathetic but altogether authentic moment complete with blood 'squibs', Hartley became troubled by the excitement that he felt at the prospect of 'making an image where it would have looked like someone really got shot. This interest in the realism of the gun shots was just so obviously foreign to the things that I'm interested in that I was angry with myself.' (25) The director decided to embrace his aversion to guns by rejecting dramatic verisimilitude in favour of a patently personal and altogether more significant approach.

Music: Having worked with Jeffrey Taylor on the New York section of *Flirt*, Hartley (again credited as the ubiquitous Ned Rifle) had seen his musical work take on a more orchestral form, or as the director describes it 'a band with horns and so on;' (26) the score for *Amateur* is a further progression in this direction using real cellists, a whole string section a double bass player and the like.

In a Hoboken studio, Hartley, who had recently attended music reading classes, and Taylor composed eight hours of recordings whilst continually replaying the movie. Relocating to a New York studio, these recordings were then finely tuned as the composers began to fit specific pieces of music to specific scenes. The string players and vocals were then added.

Tinged with the sense of longing and sadness that can be detected in much of the composed pieces found in Hartley's films, the orchestral nature of the score heightens this feeling. The piece used on the opening and closing sequences is especially affecting and is, in its relative complexity, a mark of how far Hartley had extended his abilities as a composer. Moreover, the choral quality of this piece connotes the religious aspect of the film and suggests the sense of individual tragedies and misunderstandings that are about to unfold.

There is of course the thrilling use of pop music on the soundtrack with the likes of *PJ* Harvey (later to appear in *The Book Of Life*) being used to good effect. Best of all however is Bettie Serveert's fitting *Tom Boy* which we hear blasting from Sofia's headphones after she has decided to take charge of her life.

Verdict: On a purely visual level, Hartley's most impressive and assured film at the time of completion, *Amateur* also benefits from showing a broader world view and feels like a wholly confident and mature work.

The thriller format allows the director to intelligently probe the conventions and sensibilities of the genre without prohibiting him from transposing his own preoccupations and stylised formal and thematic characteristics. The film also clearly progresses the director's on-screen grappling with questions concerning the conventions of storytelling and the demands of maintaining the illusion of cinema. To this end, *Amateur* further hastened a move away from fictional filmmaking that would become more pronounced with *Flirt*. The arguments revolving around violence and its sensationalist on-screen representation is persuasively and intelligently made and Hartley's acute sense of characterisation is as evident as ever. Hartley regulars Donovan (who combines the tricky task of exuding menace and innocence), Löwensohn and Damian Young are excellent but Huppert, despite a game approach and some fine moments, doesn't quite gel in the central role. In every sense however, a provocative and highly individual work. 3/5.

Flirt (1995)

New York, February 1993

Cast: Bill Sage (Bill), Martin Donovan (Walter), Parker Posey (Emily), Michael Imperioli (Michael), Karen Sillas (Dr. Clint), Erica Gimpel (Nurse).

Berlin, October 1994

Cast: Dwight Ewell (Dwight), Geno Lechner (Greta), Peter Fitz (Doctor), Dominik Bender (Johan), Susanna Simon (Elisabeth), Elina Löwensohn (Nurse).

Tokyo, March 1995

Cast: Miho Nikaido (Miho), Kumiko Ishizuka (Naomi), Chikako Hara (Yuki), Toshizo Fujiwara (Mr. Ozu), Hal Hartley (Hal), Masatoshi Nagase (Hal's assistant), Yutaka Matsushige (Doctor), Tomoko Fujita (Nurse).

General crew: Direction Hal Hartley, Screenplay Hal Hartley, Cinematography Michael Spiller, Production Design, Steve Rosenzweig, Music Ned Rifle and Jeffrey Taylor, Editing Steve Hamilton, 85 minutes.

Story: 'The thing to remember about *Flirt* is that the three films were made very much as three films, each one separated from the next by almost a year. Each film was completed before I even moved on to the next.' (27)

Flirt adopts the form of three films or interlinking segments/stories that ultimately combine to form a distinct whole. Plot details will be kept to a minimum to provide a general overview with contrasting details, diversions and their attendant significances later expanded upon.

In each of the above sequences the flirt of the title (respectively Bill, Dwight and Miho) is faced with the prospect of prolonged absence from their partner. Worse, a necessary trip oversees for said partner is to be spent in the company of an attractive, beautiful, witty, 'nice' former flame. The ability of the relationship to sustain itself over such distance and constraints is called into question. As the thorny question of future commitment is raised, the flirt flees, promising to return in time to escort their partner to the airport.

Unbeknownst to their lovers, the flirt, perhaps unwittingly through a solitary kiss, has become involved with another who is, to complicate matters further, married. Through the grapevine of friends and acquaintants, the flirt becomes aware of marital difficulties that have resulted through their romantic involvement and after advice from varying sources (in New York, men in a toilet, in Berlin, builders and in Tokyo, squabbling female jailbirds) attempts to interject by confronting the vengeful wronged party.

The result is a gunshot wound to the face that necessitates painful hospital treatment for the flirt and the diminishing prospect of being able to escort their long-term partner to the airport to consolidate the terms on which the relationship is to exist.

Background: Knowing that he was to edit *Amateur* on new computer technology and needing a piece of film on which to practice, Hartley revisited a ten-minute play that was performed at the Cucaracha Theatre in New York. In the play, two young men consult three articulate women – played by Hartley regulars Elina Löwensohn, Parker Posey and Adrienne Shelly – on various subjects. The piece was re-assembled to become the bathroom sequence in *Flirt* New York and a key motif in the film in terms of the ambiguities of narrative, the revealing of the processes of filmmaking and in regard to issues concerning gender roles in Japanese culture. *Flirt's* New York segment was shot in three days and edited during script revisions on *Amateur*. An attempt to make shots that were 'independent of each other; to break the confines of continuity and to tell a story in film without the need to match everything in one shot with the shot that intercuts with it,' (28) the piece was however originally envisaged as a stand alone piece.

It was during the making of the film that Hartley first conceived of the idea of interpreting the inherently typical subject matter many times over with key variations concerning the race, age, gender and sexual proclivities of the flirt in question. Hartley excitedly put the idea to longtime producer Ted Hope and even longer serving cinematographer Michael Spiller who were equally intrigued by the project. *Amateur* temporarily put the project on the backburner but it was soon resuscitated when Hope, who was as Hartley put it, 'always cooking up these schemes to raise money and travel' (29), came up with the bright idea of setting different versions in different parts of the world. Jim Jarmusch after all had mined similar terrain in *Night On Earth* to invigorating effect.

In terms of locations, little secret was made of the fact that Berlin and Tokyo were chosen because finance was forthcoming from these countries but the director was also quick to positively respond to chance and to take the step of allowing the cultural and geographical milieu of Berlin and Tokyo to help dictate visual aesthetics and how events would play out in terms of narrative and meaning as a result of transposition. Moreover, Hartley had always intended one of the segments to posit the flirt as a gay man and realised that Berlin, with its thriving gay culture and popular art scene (the Berlin sequence is very painterly both in terms of composition and in its use of the art world as a backdrop for the characters) would provide the perfect opportunity for this. Similarly, the desire of having the flirt appear as a female in one segment leant itself to Tokyo where the position of women in society would provide further interest and fresh perspectives. Hartley hoped that filming in these new locales would force him as a film-maker to 'look without preconception' and to avoid subscribing to 'some abstract notion of what a good film is' (30) in terms of linearity, verisimilitude and particularly in relation to the rendering invisible of the actual mechanics of the medium. From the clearly audible voice announcing the production details at the start of the New York sequence to other more important ways the chapter will later reveal, *Flirt* takes great pains to make transparent its conceits and it's status as a film and a piece of entertainment.

As a preface to the published *Flirt* screenplay, Tom Gunning includes a quotation from Jean Renoir, a director dear to Hartley, expressing the notion that each and every filmmaker is apt to consistently make the same film with discernible variations. It is worth noting the director's own self-imposed *La Règle du Jeu* which ran thus: 'I could move scenes around; I could delete lines of dialogue, but not add new ones; I could assign lines of dialogue to different characters. The three strangers in each city would introduce new commentary. And, just for variation, there would be a new recitation in each city.' (31) Hartley arrived at the above by recognising during the Berlin sequence that subtle differences regarding gender, sexuality had to be acknowledged and that by acknowledging them new meanings could be created.

Style and Subtext: In the case of *Flirt*, style and subtext are inextricably linked. The stylistic approach Hartley takes in foregrounding the film's processes and his juxtaposition of images, words and sounds in relation to varying environments and character conditions is also the main concern or subtext of the film; an evaluation, on behalf of both the filmmaker and the spectator, of the paradoxes of repetition and transformation and the devices by which film as a medium conjugates meaning.

To further understand how meaning is accrued from section to section it is necessary to view the structural and stylistic changes that occur in New York, Berlin and Tokyo and the degree of ambiguity in each regarding the credentials of the flirt. It is also important to note the differences in gender, race and sexuality. So, in New York, the flirt is a white heterosexual male with a genuine inability to commit to anyone and a tendency to flirt with every woman he meets; in Berlin it is a gay black man whose flirtatiousness, though extending to both men and women, is somewhat half-hearted, perhaps belying a genuine commitment to his lover, Johan. By the time we get to Tokyo we discover that the female flirt is no flirt at all but rather merely perceived of as one by her dance-troupe colleagues who claim witness to Miho's kissing of her teacher, Mr. Ozu. In New York it was merely spoken of, in Berlin it was demonstrated but here for the first time Hartley actually shows the kiss that leads to all manner of troubles and complications and it reveals Miho to be offering not amorous advances but a comforting gesture to her teacher who is depressed about the state of his marriage.

The Greek chorus of advice-givers also alters from section to section. In New York the men in the toilet (amongst them Robert Burke) offer what could be described as a more male biased litany of observations, in Berlin the builders of course serve to largely comment on the possible success of failure of the film project (see Key Moment) whilst in Tokyo, where Miho has been imprisoned for having been seen in the street with a gun, the women sharing her jail offer opposing views on the role women are expected to take in relationships in patriarchal Japanese society.

In fact, the Tokyo sequence often serves to physically show what has been only previously described or alluded to. The events leading up to the facial injury are more clearly foregrounded (in Berlin they occur off-screen leaving a certain ambiguity as to whether it is Greta, the wife of Werner, the married man Dwight has been involved with or Werner himself who fires the shot), we see Miho, surprised by two policeman, accidentally shooting herself as she tries to take the gun from Ozu's wife. Perhaps more importantly, whereas the flirts in New York and Berlin merely describe their heterosexual and homosexual sexual experiences as a means of taking their minds off their painful operations, in Tokyo there are insert shots of Miho actually enjoying sexual activity with a variety of lovers and finally Hal himself. Evidence of physical consummation is a first for the director.

Dialogue and its repetition obviously plays a major part in the film. Thus, lines such as 'you don't need to see the future if you know it's there' are not only aphoristic, aural signposts for the spectator but also another means by which Hartley explores the physical ways in which the recurring dialogue can be depicted, both increasing and diminishing in import from section to section.

In a wider context, the dialogue retains Hartley's trademark irony and humour – in the Berlin surgery the doctor offers a soothing painkiller but then adds that 'it is going to hurt anyway' – with the marked repetition from section to section evoking the deliberate rhythmic patterns and repetitiveness previously seen in the director's work. As in *Amateur* the dialogue is also again a way of describing unpleasant imagery without necessarily hav-

61

ing to reveal it; the facial injuries the flirt suffers are in each instance described in grimacing detail – 'your lip is split in three places' – but never actually shown.

The film of course retains Hartley's keen visual characteristics, such as the attention to composition and framing and an irreverence, particular in the editing phase for establishing shots and continuity but it is also important to note the ways in which each section visually contrast, reflecting the director's own response to the environment in which he filmed. The New York section is understandably the most recognisably Hartleyian with its noisy street-sounds, bold colours and bar culture. In Berlin, Hartley films in wintry blues and grays and there is a somewhat austere quality in terms of composition as if in deference to the city's reputation as a hotbed of culture. This shooting of the sequences in the tenement flats where Greta and Werner live are especially diverting with one sequence – Greta's daughter framed in a doorway against a walled backdrop – seemingly being culled from another era. This notion is perhaps gently subverted however by the noises of the modern game machine Greta's daughter plays with. With its obvious interest in and reverence for dance, choreography and experimental theatre – traditions for which Japan is famed – the Tokyo section is certainly the most exciting and dynamic. It is also the segment with the least dialogue, in part a result of Hartley's unease with the language but also a reflection of the director's desire to relate through images and to communicate how dialogue and indeed the lack of 'can be compelling by virtue of its success or its failure at communication.' (32) It is precisely because thoughts are not always made explicit in the Tokyo section that misconceptions and misunderstandings occur. The director seems to be liberated by the street culture in Japan and captures the bright neon and lantern lit cityscapes with an increased use of tracking and panning shots and a generally more vibrant camera. This vibrancy is also evident in the interior sequences, specifically the rehearsal sequence choreographed by Yoshito Ohno, but also during the moment where Miho is tracked by the two policemen in the bookstore where the camera pans back and forth across the aisles. Hartley feels the Japanese section of the film exists as 'the best work I've done.' (33)

It's also interesting to note that not only does Miho read aloud a passage from a book (in each section in fact this act takes place), thus allowing Hartley to retain his fondness for this action but that we also catch a glimpse of the younger policemen perusing a pornographic magazine. Another observation regarding the roles ascribed to women within Japanese society, plus a further footnote to Hartley's continued wider interest concerning the objectification of the female body. An earlier shot from the Berlin section featuring a naked woman during a fashion shoot is more questionable and again blurs the line in the director's career between questioning exploitation and being guilty of it.

Economy now dictates an at best cursory listing of further stylistic and thematic Hartley motifs that can be detected in the film. Already noted is the assuredness of the composition and the willingness to adopt an elliptical approach to narrative and image (witness the way in which Bill explains his romantic involvement with a married woman; with his back to the camera, revealing the information in a series of jump-cuts), there is also the regular violent outbursts and slaps and punches, the inventive juxtaposition of sound and image and the conversations that endlessly skirt around each other before arriving back at their starting point ('what will you tell him?' 'What do you want me to tell him?' 'I don't want to tell you what to do,' 'that would be the same thing.'). Also added to the list: a fascination with relationships in all their ambiguity, trust and commitment, betrayal of same, an interest in politics (Miho's bag sports a CND sticker) and, in the final section at least, strong, independent female characters.

Key Moment: Inspired by the street where he was living in Berlin, Kantstrasse, Hartley decided to make the strangers who comment upon Dwight's possible modes of action not only builders – the blue collar sensibility again? – but unlikely philosophers. It becomes clear that their analysis of Dwight's situation and the fact that elements from the New York sequence are being repeated with slight inflections to reflect different dynamics have far wider implications and are a means of making transparent the central conceit of the project. After explicit reference to the fact that the audience is privy to a game, an inventive piece of entertainment, the trio also acknowledges the presence of a director, debating his ability to pull off the project.

Builder 1: 'The filmmaker's project is to compare the changing dynamics of the same situation in different milieus.'

Builder 2: 'And you don't think he'll succeed?'

Builder 1: 'I don't know, it's too early to tell but I think he will fail.'

Builder 3: 'Yes he will fail. He has already failed but in this case the failure is interesting.'

The discussion reveals the processes at play in the making of cinema and toys with the notion that the medium is based purely on illusion. The next logical step in foregrounding the actuality of film and the fact that *Flirt*, like any film is a construction (further, it should not go unnoted that all the central protagonists retain their forenames) was Hartley appearing in the film as himself, a sacrifice he made for the Tokyo section; 'I didn't really like being before the camera. And I didn't act. I just did things and recited the dialogue.' (34) Moreover, a can of film Hartley is working on is clearly visible, the title on the can? *Flirt*.

An engagingly honest moment, the above discussion also speaks volumes about the conception Hartley has of his audience – who are after all at this very moment invited to 'assess the success or failure of the movie' (35) and their willingness to see him stumble and falter in pursuit of a personal means of expression. This philosophy of course also applies and then some to Hartley's own requirements of himself as a filmmaker and his desire that his failures be just as interesting as his successes.

Music: It was on the original short piece *Flirt NYC* that Hartley/Rifle and Jeffrey Taylor began to move towards a score that adopted orchestral musical qualities. The music in the film's first segment errs toward simplicity (it's largely piano and synthesizer led) whilst hinting at the more complex identities Hartley's scores would assume post *Amateur*.

It's fair to say that the compositions for the Berlin and Tokyo segments strive, like the film's visual aesthetic, to capture something of the cities themselves. To this end, it's amongst Hartley's most eclectic scores. There is also the inclusion of geographically disparate tracks such as the rhythmic and beautiful *Tavasz Tavasz* by popular Hungarian folk singer Marta Sebestyen. The piece closes Berlin and segues to Tokyo.

Banding these two sequences together in more general terms, the variations on the original flirt theme have become more deeply thought and elaborately constructed, utilising a sophisticated menagerie of instruments. Again, the mood the music captures is predominantly thoughtful and a little mournful – with the exception of the piece used in the background in the discussion over Miho's fidelity between Hal and his assistant which resembles the noir/jazz of Barry Adamson – though the final end credit piece has a suitably more celebratory feel to it.

Verdict: Hartley described the film as resembling a school assignment and there's no denying its rigorous experimental nature. But, the director also strives to make sure that *Flirt* is an ultimately entertaining experience, maintaining a playful balance between formal inquiry, intellectual pursuits and the exploration of transgressive methods of storytelling. Importantly, Hartley avoids the mistake of confusing indulgence for adventure. Offering further evidence of the director's belief that 'film is essentially graphic' (36) and auguring a move even further away from convention to shorter, non-narrative pieces, *Flirt* remains Hartley's most experimental feature to date. Conversely, in closing it is worth considering the sense of closure at the end of the film – the re-establishment of the relationship between Miho and Hal – and the uncharacteristic move toward romantic resolution. Without wishing to blur the boundary between art and reality, there is an added poignancy in light of the fact that Nikaido and Hartley were to marry in real life. Of course, in the New York and Berlin sections the central relationship is left in a more ambiguous state and so Tokyo's denouement could be seen purely in terms of the interest in contingency and its connection to meaning. However, the sense that a truly emotional investment is leant to both the material and the characters lingers. 4/5.

Henry Fool (1997)

Cast: Thomas Jay Ryan (Henry Fool), James Urbaniak (Simon Grim), Parker Posey (Fay), Maria Porter (Mary), James Saito (Mr. Deng), Kevin Corrigan (Warren), Liam Aiken (Ned), Miho Nikaido (Gnoc Deng), Nicholas Hope (Father Hawkes), Chuck Montgomery (Angus James).

Crew: Direction Hal Hartley, Screenplay Hal Hartley, Cinematography Michael Spiller, Production Design Steve Rosenzweig, Music Hal Hartley and Jim Coleman, Editing Steve Hamilton, 137 minutes.

Story: Shy, sexually naive garbage man Simon Grim leads an oppressed, downbeat New Jersey existence. Saddled with a manic- depressive mother and a promiscuous, work-shy sister, Kay, Simon finds little release amongst the inhabitants of his blue-collar neighborhood who largely treat him with violent disdain.

Grim's world is turned on its head by the arrival of Henry Fool (as ever, Hartley's choice of names are telling), a rebellious, articulate, confident and enigmatic stranger with a penchant for classic literature. The charismatic but disheveled Henry moves into Simon's decrepit basement and discloses to his enraptured landlord that he is close to completing his lifework, his *Confession*, a series of books – part philosophy, part literature – that are going to 'blow a hole in the world.' Henry, who it later transpires has served a lengthy jail term for sexual transgressions with a 13-year-old girl, extols the virtues of creative expression and soon Simon is compelled to put pen to paper.

Though betraying Simon's inexperience and lack of education, the result, written in iambic pentameter, suggests to Henry that his initiate has natural talent. When Henry brazenly posts the poem in the local Asian owned store, the results range from an outbreak in song from the store owner's silent daughter, to accusations of pornography from the conservative-minded locals, one of whom, Warren, has recently begun canvassing for popular right wing election candidate, Owen Feer.

Increasingly confident of his abilities, Simon gives up his job to concentrate on his writing, forcing Kay to mend her wayward lifestyle. Encouraged by Henry, Simon visits Fool's friend, publisher, Angus James, who happens to be keen to unearth new poetry as a means of staving off the threat to publishing posed by the internet. A kindly aide, Laura, persuades James to read the work, which he dismisses. The assistant also divulges that Henry was a janitor at the publishers.

Simon returns to find that Henry has seduced his mother and that Kay has posted the poem on the Internet. The result is immediate coverage and a heated international debate that rages in the media between figures as disparate as Camille Paglia and the Pope as to whether the work is representative of challenging new art or merely contributes to the systematic destruction of values and morality. Henry then seduces Kay, the pair nosily coupling in the basement whilst Simon's mother silently slips into the bathroom to take her own life. Kay and Henry are married.

Angus James seizes the notoriety surrounding Simon's poem and offers him a significant publishing advance. As a mark of allegiance, Simon refuses unless James also prints Henry's *Confessions*. James refuses after reading the work, which is totally without merit. Simon signs the publishing contract, confronting Henry with his actions on the birth of Henry's son, Ned. Amidst accusations of betrayal, Simon and Henry part.

Five years later, Henry is living a life of smothering domesticity and setting a terrible example to his son by drinking and smoking heavily. Henry finds himself once again in a compromising position with a minor, Pearl, who offers sexual intercourse in return for the murder of her abusive father, Warren. Spurning the offer, Henry does however confront Warren, accidentally killing him in the resulting stand-off.

In an attempt to help his father escape the attentions of the police, Ned tracks down the successful and revered Simon to the plush New York apartment he shares with Laura. On the eve of flying to Stockholm to receive the Nobel Prize, Simon gives Henry his passport and encourages him to flee. On the runway Henry is faced with an arduous choice, a flight to freedom or the return to the family he has come to love and a fight to clear his name?

Background: 'Even in the infancy of my creative development as a writer and storyteller, there was this inclination to tell a big story about the education and adventures of a particular person. Henry was there at the beginning – I just never knew what to do with him.' (37) After returning to a character he had toyed with in college and marrying it to the tale of a man from a blue-collar background who notches up huge creative achievements but still somehow finds his life tinged with regret, Hartley drew upon a recent personal experience for the central kernel of the film; Simon's promise of allegiance to Henry's work, an allegiance he is forced to sacrifice in order to grasp the publishing opportunity presented him. Hartley's own championing of somebody else's work, a misguided act of friendship as opposed to a true belief in the quality of the work Hartley was endorsing, informed this issue of creative and personal integrity.

Far wider in scope and scale than Hartley's previous work, that it was during the writing stages influenced by big, literary works such as *Don Quixote* and *Faust* should come as little surprise. Hartley also admits to having drawn on a lot of 'classic models of epic films, including *Dr Zhivago* and *Lawrence Of Arabia*, with the intention of creating a story like that in my own medium and my own mode.' (38)

If Hartley was able to use his name, misguided or not, as a means of attracting attention to the work of another, it, and his not insignificant reputation as one of the U.S independent scene's most consistent director's was of little worth when it came to securing finance for the ambitious project. *Flirt* may have been a creative and critical success but it had only minimal commercial impact and without substantial foreign investment, Hartley, taking a Producer role and with his True Fiction company acting as one of the production companies, was forced to once again work on a very tight budget; a creative discipline he had long since mastered. Although a film larger in scale and with many more characters, *Henry Fool* – at the outset described as a relatively conventional story told by conventional means but about unconventional subjects – was made for about $1 million, comparatively speaking the same amount as his second feature, *Trust*. Hartley remained sanguine about the vagaries of film financing and any fashionability his name may or may not have: 'the climate changes and it changes all the dynamics of the assumed value of an artist's work...business is business. I just try not to take it personally' (39)

It's also worth noting that the film's ambitious scale may have in part been due not only to the literary influences and the film's epic aspirations – it is the director's longest film by some margin and Hartley has since joked that he envisioned the film spawning *Star Wars* like sequels – but due to the writer-director's striving to create a film less driven by the quick-fire, winning dialogue with which he is commonly associated and more by the seismic shifts, sways and progressions in the lives of a multi-character drama. Though written with unequalled fervor, Hartley then systematically went through and removed much of the punctuation so that the actor's would be less reliant on Hartley's trademark rhythm and witticisms and would imbue the lines with their own cadence and nuances. Perhaps the least Hartley-like of all his screenplays – that's not to say it doesn't also contain characteristic comic and aphoristic traits – it nonetheless netted Hartley Best Screenplay at the 1998 Cannes Film Festival.

Style: There is much in *Henry Fool* that bears Hartley's signature. Geoff Andrew describes the film as offering a summation of the director's key preoccupations: trust, oppressive, dysfunctional families (Simon's absent father is described by Hartley as having been killed in Vietnam), the pressure to conform and accept financial and moral responsibility, reactionary political attitudes, the role of rumour and the relationship between a well-schooled mentor and a less educated, knowledge-hungry disciple. Visually the film also bears characteristic Hartley hallmarks: a pervading, flab-free visual economy and no nonsense approach to editing (there is however an increase in the use of dissolves but the absence of identifying establishing shots remains), and, courtesy of Spiller and regular gaffer W.F Stubblefield, a tonal and compositional assurance. This is particularly evident in regard to the relationship between people and their environment (witness the scenes involving both Simon and Henry in garbage central and the shot where we first see Henry approaching). There's also an inventive juxtaposition of sound and image, especially in the scene where Warren's partner puts her hands over her ears to drown out the sound of fist on flesh; the film cuts to silence. The sound in the film also reflects the urban environment; whole swathes of dialogue are often drowned out by the sound of planes and general street noises. An important aesthetic no doubt but also a reflection of the film's limited budget that would have made re-shoots and re-recording prohibitive.

However, the film clearly differs from the director's previous features in numerous key structural ways, some of which are directly related to the sources from which Hartley took his inspiration and the scope he was searching for. It is never easy trying to define a Hal Hartley film in terms of genre as he pays only cursory attention to it. But, as previous chapters have shown, he has kind of shoehorned his work into the melodrama, the road-movie and the thriller format. *Henry Fool* is a little different. The enigmatic stranger arriving in town with seismic effect most closely approximates the motifs of the Western and the film – the aforementioned arrival shot of Henry in which he emerges from beyond the horizon is telling in this regard – certainly contains echoes of two classic oaters, *Shane* and *The Searchers*. Henry's 'I go where I will' line is another pointer. The director has himself cited Ford's masterly picture as an influence, specifically in connection to a man at odds with society and the character of Henry indeed mirrors that of Ethan Edwards in numerous ways, most generally in terms of the criminal past and the troubled psyche they both share. It's also worth remembering that Hartley studied the genre and retains a particular fondness for it.

Miniaturist in formal terms it may be but *Henry Fool* structurally is indeed epic in scope. It features an enormous amount of major characters, more than in previous work and covers a six-year time frame. As well as capturing personal change and progression on an internal and individual level, Hartley also shows the very real effects of the passages of time on the film's subjects in external terms. They grow-up (Ned, the last homage to Ned Rifle? and Pearl), grow old (a withered looking Fay) and they take jobs they don't like and stick at them to pay the bills. People die and the landscape around them changes as new fads; nightclubs and loud music, replace old ones; espresso drinking and in-store poetry readings. A political campaign is fought, and lost in a neighborhood that grows increasingly ugly.

In much of Hartley's work the relationship between a teacher and an initiate and the ensuing process of cultural enlightenment occurs between a man and a woman with resulting romantic tension. In *Henry Fool* the central relationship is between two men and it is this dynamic that drives the narrative. Commentators have described the relationship and indeed the general scope of the film as Shakespearean in nature and Hartley has admitted similarities between Henry and Simon and Falstaff and Prince Henry (Hal). Incidentally, newcomers to the Hartley fold, Urbaniak, playing uptight and repressed and Jay Ryan, charismatic, turbulent, dangerous and inspiring are mesmerising in the central roles.

It is also true that whilst Hartley's central protagonists are sketched with a certain moral or psychological ambiguity; think *Trust's* Matthew Slaughter, *Simple Men's* Bill or *Amateur's* Thomas, the character of Henry is by far the director's most ambiguous, complex and contradictory. Described as being written as a consideration of 'what happens if the most untrustworthy person in town were also the best,' (40)

Henry is an unapologetically troubling creation who evokes Dennis Potter's satanic intruder in *Brimstone and Treacle*. Witty, erudite, educated and honest, he's also a sexual predator, prone to moments of 'weakness' and apt to take advantage of both adults and children. Henry's cultural integrity and acumen is admirable but somewhat undermined by the revelation that his own artistic pursuits are worthless. Riffing on the angel/devil dichotomy (Jay Ryan would play the devil in Hartley's next work, *The Book Of Life*), Henry is intermittently revealed as a man capable of goodness and honest acts but Hartley truly tests notions of identification by providing Henry with so murky a sexual past.

For so long averted, 'raw, ugly consummation' (41) is finally revealed in abundance in *Henry Fool*. In part to demonstrate Simon's sexual revulsion and divorce from the sensual world, it is also part of the film's general bawdy, Rabelaisian humour, something we have not come to expect from

Hartley's work. There are of course other elements of humour in the film such as Simon's wondering how Henry knows his name (he is wearing a name badge) that are more in keeping with the director's wry, ironic sensibility but episodes such as Simon's vomiting on a couple having sex, Henry's sonorous bowel movements and the frequently earthy dialogue as demonstrated by Fay's 'God, I wanna get fucked' may seem alien to the world of a Hartley movie. This is especially true for those critics and detractors who feel that he creates purely antiseptic, precious environments for his characters to inhabit. I have argued elsewhere that I do not feel this to be the case; such charges that his films do not deal with the realistic contemporary milieu all too easily overlook the dark, contentious issues with which he deals and the frequent violent outbursts that recur, but there is certainly a sense in the film that the director is being deliberately outrageous as if to confront these criticisms. Hartley, who has professed that he is not himself averse to a little gross-out humour, highlighted such moments as a further attempt to confound the expectations of his audience – as he did so memorably on a structural level with *Flirt* – and to answer his own question regarding the desire of an audience to see sex and violence on screen, 'how can I make the kind of movie I want to make and still provide these things? I'll try to fit the violence, the sex, the grossness into my world.' (42)

The locations in which Hartley filmed obviously influenced the visual tone. Shooting on location in the rundown Woodside, Queens, area in New York and picking none too glamorous settings such as squalid basements (the predominantly red lighting on Henry, lit from below, is superb in these sequences), garbage dumps and seedy bars, Hartley continued the exercise he had learned on *Flirt*; the capacity to respond to his physical environment and the act of regarding it as if it were a different planet. Gone are the mirrored city surfaces of *Amateur*; in their place a more muted palette and the favoring of sombre, almost drab blacks, browns and greens. Hartley has stated that this palette was not specifically imposed but merely a reflection of what was already there. Having motioned toward a less static camera on more recent projects as his budgets grew, Hartley returned to more stationary use of camera on *Henry Fool*, again demonstrating the correlation between aesthetics and economy. *Cinéma verité* is cited as an influence on the back to basics, pared down visual style of the film. Again a budgetary consideration, Hartley returns to the intense, often claustrophobic concentration upon faces that dominated his first two features, mixing it up by retaining his customary oblique use of angles – the first shot of the *World of Donuts* eaterie is particularly startling – and askance way of viewing people and places. In certain scenes people seem to literally intrude or stumble into the frame, Hartley's attempt to 'get that excitement you get in documentary, but without sacrificing the evidence of formal construction.' (43)

In regard to the highly ambiguous ending of the film, we are used to seeing Hartley resolve things in somewhat cryptic fashion, normally involving a male protagonist taking the choice to face justice in order to revive his romantic interest, but the ending of *Henry Fool* is deliberately open to multiple interpretations. The published script clearly has Henry about to become a fugitive and an exiled father and husband by joining the departing plane for Stockholm. Geographically speaking the director also shot this ending but when Hartley's brother pointed out that there was a question mark over the direction in which Henry is heading, i.e. towards or away from the plane, Hartley again erred toward a lack of closure, removing a key shot of a stewardess waving Henry on to. Hartley is tight-lipped on the subject, claiming that 'the question mark is good.' (44) Personally, I believe that Henry is running back to his family and to face the music about the circumstances in which he killed Warren. As such, it's a further significant step towards Henry's moral re-birth and a gesture of the emotional investment Hartley has placed in this troubled and troubling character, about whom we are left to form our own ethical conclusions.

Subtext: Many of the notable thematic concerns of the film have already been alluded to in the above section, as have their recurrence in the director's work. Some are worthy of further comment, whilst other, newer observations also need to be covered.

A keen observer of male treatment of women and issues of sexuality, Hartley considerably darkens the terrain in *Henry Fool*. Warren is revealed to be a habitual abuser; the bruises on Pearl's mother are there for all to see. As an aside, the violence is also generally more abundant, vicious and symptomatic of suffering and less a humorous punctuation mark and wry comment on human behaviour. The violence is graphically suggested both visually: the victimisation of Simon, Fay's pouring of scolding water on his back and the stylised but nonetheless quite sickening fight between Warren and Henry; and through descriptive dialogue: Henry's mordant description of the time he staved off a beating by threatening to take out an eye of one of his tormentors. Convicted for his past indiscretion with a minor, Henry's raging and transgressive libido is finally tempered by marriage to Fay, whose earlier promiscuousness can largely be attributed to boredom. Incidentally, I read Fay as one of the more positive aspects of the film, swapping indolence for a role as a supportive, if wary mother. However, the film largely portrays the woman's lot as an unhappy one; there's the silenced storeowner's daughter, the abused mothers and the much-pawed strippers in the titty bar.

Intended as 'an accurate picture of what America is,' (45) *Henry Fool* also strikes hard against right-wing reactionary politics. The directionless Warren – who continues the sobering theme of child-molestation – discovers politics and dedicates his energies to congressman Owen Feer's (another symbolic surname) political campaign for election. Immediately pegged as a Nazi by Fay, Feer preaches racial intolerance and cultural bigotry, winning support with his ability to take 'complicated issues and totally simplify them.' Though ultimately defeated, his ignorant, back-to-basic manifestos appear tempting to the economically dispossessed, blame hungry Neanderthals, as epitomised by Warren.

Central to the film and a further exploration of the notion of cultural bigotry are the diverse responses Simon's poem prompts and the media frenzy it incites. Deemed as pure pornography by some, it is defended by cultural commentators and liberal minded freethinkers, Camille Paglia (appearing as herself) amongst them, as 'the authentic trashing voice of modern America.' It is telling of course that Hartley deliberately does not reveal the content of Simon's work, or for that matter Henry's. This was so as to avoid allowing the audience to judge the works as good or bad art but instead observe the way that artistic worth is measured purely by the reaction, positive or negative, it attracts. Questions of profitability and the correlation between celebrity and commercial worth and novelty and originality also abound.

The film continues Hartley's interest in literature and reverence for books whilst developing further the role technology plays in shaping our world and the way we receive and control information. Hartley toyed with this theme and *Amateur* and would return to it in *The Book Of Life*. Angus James' publishing empire is threatened by the possibilities offered by the internet; as his advisors inform him, books will soon be a thing of the past with people consuming literature on-line. The uses and abuses of the Internet and issues of censorship are further explored in the film's examination of the wild fire effect when Simon's poem is broadcast Online by Fay and the myriad potential the Internet offers in terms of pornographic material.

Previously a footnote in Hartley's work, the subject of religion, and more importantly the sustenance of faith are given lengthy consideration in the form of the doubting Father Hawkes (played with ecclesiastical irreverence by *Bad Boy Bubby's* Nicholas Hope). Like *Simple Men's* lovelorn sheriff, the padre is obviously ill suited to his profession.

Key Moment: Previous chapters in this book have tended toward moments that demonstrate Hartley's visual sensibilities. In *Henry Fool there* are many individual instances that could be chosen for this effect, such as the juxtaposition of Henry and Fay fucking whilst Fay's mother slits her wrists, or the beguiling moment where, after helping Henry escape, the key members of the community walk away from Fay who is framed behind imposing railings. However, I am instead going to extract a very short, staccato exchange between Henry and Mr. Deng that distills the overall tone and gloomy, disquieting mood of the film into a single moment.

Perched on a seat outside his former convenience store, now a noisy club, Mr. Deng is distractedly watching a sports game on a small portable television. Henry approaches, registers the action and with similar disinterest asks, 'Who's winning?' 'Nobody' is the reply.

It's a simple, understated moment but one of extreme and rather ominous lucidity in regard to the apathetic, resignedly waning and oppressively banal environment Hartley's film calculatedly portrays. Henry repeatedly states his belief that it is a 'shitty' world; Hartley shares the sentiment.

Music: Working again with Jim Coleman, Hartley, as a mark of his increasing confidence and the creative freedom accorded him by the sensibilities of *Flirt*, comes out of the shadow of Ned Rifle and composes and performs the music under his own name. Several pieces are performed solo (Hartley's piano/synthesizer skills have come on leaps and bounds), others are performed with the backing of just Jim Coleman or the band Ryful, comprised of Hartley, Coleman, Hub Moore, Bill Dobrow and Lydia Kavanagh.

The music largely continues the direction displayed in the composer's previous two outings, erring towards more complex sounds that utilise a cross-section of instruments, or at least a machine that duplicates them. The opening and closing title sequences credit Prokovief and have a weight, tone and sense of import in keeping not only with the scale of the film but the lingering menace and contradictions inherent in the character of Henry Fool. Other pieces are more simplistic, scaled-down affairs, effective in capturing the inescapable melancholy at the heart of the film. The piece composed for the mother's suicide is amongst the most accomplished and emotionally engaging Hartley has written.

There is less use of the work of other artists with the Ryful providing the more rock-orientated numbers that seem to speak of abandonment, romantic woe and a thirst for beer. The characters in *Henry Fool* drink a lot of beer.

Verdict: Defined as mature, ambitious and progressive upon release by those not normally enamored by the director's work, *Henry Fool* certainly displays all these qualities. I have argued throughout this book that the environment of a Hal Hartley film has, from *Kid* onwards, always been imbued with a realism and an awareness of the unpleasantness of the modern world; Hartley has never avoided the underbelly, in *Henry Fool* he simply shoves it to the fore. So whilst maturity and ambition are qualities I have always discerned in Hartley's oeuvre (and I do here wish to distance myself from those who praised the film believing it to be in opposition to the director's earlier works) it is a fair point to concede that *Henry Fool*, though not without a both devilish and satirical humour, is his most consistently dark film to-date. Re-viewing, I was struck by just how powerful it seems and how I initially underrated it and failed to grasp its cogency. Certainly not as assiduously charming as the early films, all things considered, *Henry Fool* just might be Hal Hartley's best work to-date. 4/5.

The Book Of Life (1998)

Cast: Martin Donovan (Jesus Christ), PJ Harvey (Magdalena), Thomas Jay Ryan (Satan), Miho Nikaido (Edie), Dave Simonds (Dave)

Crew: Direction Hal Hartley, Screenplay Hal Hartley, Cinematography Jim Denault, Production Design Andy Biscontini, Music Various, Editing Steve Hamilton, 60 minutes.

Story: December 31st, 1999. A downcast Jesus Christ arrives at JFK airport with his loyal assistant Magdalena in tow. It's the eve of a new Millennium and with the media predicting the end of the world, people are a little nervous. Frankly, the omens are not good.

An emissary from God, Jesus grudgingly sets about his father's business. That business of course the judging of the living and the dead and the collection of 144,000 good souls that will be spared the horror of the Apocalypse. However, once in possession of the all powerful *The Book Of Life*, a laptop containing the names of the fortunate and not-so fortunate souls and the software to unleash such undesirables as warfare, famine, pestilence, slaughter and the like, Jesus begins to suffer a crisis of faith that leads him to question his father's vengeful selection methods. God's attorneys are forced to adopt a hard-line approach; Jesus faces banishment from the Kingdom of Heaven.

Meanwhile, Satan is also collecting souls. To this end he offers Dave, a perennial gambler and committed atheist the winning lottery ticket in return for the soul of Edie, a kind-hearted waitress with an unquenchable desire to do good. Each good soul stolen away from Jesus is one more personal victory for Satan who is still out to settle old scores with his former employer. Jesus is persuaded by Magdalena to intervene and a trade-off is offered: *The Book Of Life* in return for Edie's soul. Will Jesus accept and at what cost to the future of human kind?

Background: Hartley had been working for two years on a play about Christian Millennialists, the central focus of which was their anticipation of Christ's judgment of the living and the dead, when the offer to make *The Book Of Life* arose. The offer came from French companies Haut Et Court and La Sept ARTE who were putting together a series of film projects to cover the impending 2000 Millennium. Under the banner of *2000 Seen By*, film directors from each corner of the globe were asked to transcribe on film what the impending Millennium signified on a personal level and how it related to the anxieties and hopes of their fellow countrymen. Other directors taking part in the ambitious undertaking included Walter Salles (*Mid-*

night) and Alain Berliner (*The Wall*). Struggling to adapt his ideas to the theatrical medium and enthusiastic about working within the constraints of the project in terms of both the subject matter and the restricted budget, Hartley seized the opportunity to embrace the aesthetics of digital video.

Collectively, the films were made for television broadcast – Hartley's was the American entry – and the director was enthused by the playful challenges his controversial re-telling of the Apocalypse would present to US TV programmers. The funding problems Hartley had encountered with *Henry Fool* had proved to be depressingly ominous and the film fared relatively poorly both in Europe and America. With funding for features harder to come by the ever inventive and resourceful director sought fresh creative challenges and adapted to the economic environment by turning his hand to shorter, more experimental projects. Nothing if not realistic about the artistic environment and his place in it, Hartley played down the potentially controversial reaction some envisioned to *The Book Of Life* by suggesting that the film 'will go unnoticed by any significant portion of the American public.' (46) In Britain, *The Book Of Life* aired, appropriately, on New Year's Eve, 1999.

Before proceeding, a quick comment on the film's iconic casting of PJ Harvey in the role of Magdalena. Hartley had used the music of the widely admired West Country singer on *Amateur* – their creative relationship continues to this day with Hartley acknowledged on the singer's recent *Stories From The City, Stories From The Sea* LP – and was immediately receptive to the intense Catholic imagery in her songs of tortured love. 'I looked for the harmonies between materials: a character Magdalena, a person (persona) Harvey. It seemed the only natural direction to go in.' (47) This sensibility is again reflected in the scene where Magdalena goes into a record store and sings to one of Harvey's own songs. The sequence – which concludes with the sound being removed from the image – is another example of the director drawing attention to the tools of cinema. Similarly in regard to this sense of harmony between materials, Donovan was welcomed aboard as Christ, being the 'most lapsed Catholic' (48) the director knew. Having explored the Angel/Devil dichotomy in *Henry Fool*, Thomas Jay Ryan was finally given full Satanic license. The black eye he sports is not the work of make-up but the effects of a late night drinking session the night before filming. The actor and director felt it was somehow in keeping with character and so it remained.

Style: Again keenly aware of the intimate relationship between aesthetics and economy, Hartley eschewed trying to replicate 35mm film and instead embraced the aesthetics of the digital video format (a relatively inexpensive and decidedly mobile mode of production), making them the key visual characteristic of *The Book Of Life*. The resulting film is defined by a blurring of images and colours, possessing a kinetic jolt as a result of the largely hand-held photography of Jim Denault. The crisp precision of earlier work is replaced by a hypnotic, at first dizzying sense of urgency in keeping with the film's concern with a lack of time and impending destruction. This is clearly illustrated by the opening, hurried arrival of Jesus Christ and Magdalena and their transportation by ubiquitous yellow cab car through various brightly lit inner city tunnels before arriving (via uncharacteristic establishing shot of a highway sign) in downtown Manhattan. Thrillingly set to the tune of Takako Minekawa's *1.666666*, the opening sequence also intimately captures the harangued expressions of Jesus and Magdalena – the film makes frequent use of intense facial close-up's – as they speed toward their dreaded task. Moreover, in terms of genre, the film appropriately has the feel of a snappily paced thriller, from the use of Christ's portentous voiceover ('It was the morning of December 31st 1999 when I returned at last to judge the living and the dead') to the frantic pursuit of Christ by Satan through the streets of New York. Again, the digital format allows for this increased sense of mobility. As Satan dashes forward in search of his quarry, background buildings and figures merge, blur and distort. Later in the film, once the terrible retribution is avoided, Hartley captures a very different environment to the largely deserted, rain-sodden streets of the film's beginning. As the brightly attired denizens of New York City rush to embrace the new Millennium, taking to the streets to shop, skate and generally mingle, there's an even more intensified rush of movement and colour and the neon bright images further blur and distort. This sense of distortion was primary in the director's mind, with Hartley comparing the effect he was after to the role sonic distortion and amplified feedback plays in popular music. This is replicated aurally as well as visually in certain scenes such as the discussion between Jesus and Magdalena prior to the retrieval of the laptop, which is set to a background of screeching feedback.

The film's general production values are also impressive and inventive. Befittingly, Satan wears a red shirt throughout and is often filmed bathed in settings that are defined by a Hellish red glow. Overall, the film has an ethereal quality with much of the shooting taking place in artificially lit hotels and office buildings. This is again in keeping with Hartley's need to make the most of his environment in terms of budget but is also again reflective of the overall tone of the film and the fact that it captures a society increasingly immersed in modernity and the dual pursuits of work and leisure. The director is also inventive in the sequence in which Christ begins opening the book of life and unlocking the seals of the next stage of the Apocalypse. Filmed on a desolate rooftop that evokes Christ's misgivings and inner turmoil, the presence of The Empire State Building is a striking background that further underlines the magnitude of what is about to be destroyed in the name of Christianity.

Whilst tension is economically created by having the seals that unleash the next stages of the Apocalypse being unlocked on the screen of a laptop, the director also effectively creates the horror of impending destruction and violence through a trusty recourse to dialogue. The sonorous tones of a preacher intone on the radio airwaves what humans can expect once God wreaks his wrath: 'It will be ugly...carnage like you've never seen before.' Hartley's production designer, who does a pretty passable impression of William S. Burroughs, provides the voice of the preacher.

Elsewhere, Hartley's dialogue is typically astute, capturing the despairing qualities associated with 20th Century existence and the loneliness and disappointment we are often forced to endure. As Satan remarks of Dave: 'A lonely directionless human forever at the mercy of your own insignificant hopes and dreams.' But, Hartley also intended to be irreverent and downright funny and as ever there are some wonderfully comic lines in the film. Complaining that he's been 'misunderstood,' Satan is reminded by Jesus that, 'you didn't quit, you were fired.' Cowered by Jesus' mighty reputation, Dave introduces himself by saying 'I'd just like to apologise for my entire existence.'

Elsewhere too there's evidence of Hartley's at times mischievous sense of humour and general sensibility. Jesus and Magdalena check into the hotel as Mr. and Mrs. D.W Griffith. Hartley had increasingly referenced directors in his work; there's a Mr. Ozu in *Flirt* and an Officer Buñuel in *Henry Fool*. Also deployed is an irreverent treatment of violence, the moment where Jesus jabs Satan in the gut is fantastic, and a highly comedic office shoot-out between the Christian attorneys (as a profession attorneys are given short shrift) and invading Mormons that has fun with the conventions of on-screen shoot-out's.

Subtext: Having already touched upon the central subject of the film – to an extent a dictate of the *2000 Seen By* project – and the way in which Hartley personally re-interprets the coming of the Apocalypse, it's worth again noting the role of religion in the director's work – here it obviously appears more prominently than previously – and how the film drastically questions some of the central tenets of Catholicism. To all intents and purposes, this is reflected in Jesus' reluctance to not only pass judgment on the living and the dead but his open dispute with his father's more vengeful sensibilities; 'My father is an angry God. To him the law is everything. To this day attorneys are his favourites.' Even Satan, who attempts to persuade Jesus to coin a new religion with him, is wary of God's bloodlust and his apparent contempt and lack of mercy for his subjects, observing, 'God's tolerance for you stupid human beings has reached its end.'

Moreover, the compassionate Jesus, who refuses to destroy humanity because he is 'addicted' to it, casts aspersion on the criteria on which people are judged by the laws of the Catholic religion, angrily claiming to 'hate their open and closed door policy.' The film is also at pains to highlight the hypocrisy of Catholicism, capturing Jesus as, though admittedly loath, he 'rises to the occasion and lies' to the suffering souls of those slaughtered in the name of God. *The Book Of Life* also presents a more multi-faceted, non-simplistic portrait of religion and to this end has characters that are also Buddhists, Mormons and Atheists. Hartley also makes intelligent parallels between religion and the world of marketing, a profession in which Satan professes himself to be an expert, the central art of that particular trade being an ability to convince people of what is good for them.

When, in the film's final moments Jesus throws the Book of Life into the river from a departing ferry – a profoundly moving image – the film's questioning of the failings and foibles of mankind is extended to consider its future in a final, impassioned voiceover. 'In a hundred years will they all be born in test tubes or perhaps evolve through computers to become disembodied intelligence machines...will they still believe life is sacred?'

This preoccupation with evolution and genetics of course underscores the film's interest in technological evolution and the role technology plays in our lives. The fact that the all-important book is actually a laptop continues the direction Hartley envisioned with regard to publishing in *Henry Fool*. It is of course also a novel way of imagining the onslaught of the Apocalypse, the director actually managing to render the opening of Mac OS software riveting and dramatic. Comic mileage is also drawn from this when Satan, a technical Luddite is unable to open the book and takes it to a repairer only to be informed that the make is foreign, 'probably Egyptian,' ancient and with an expired warranty.

As ever with a Hal Hartley film, love and troubled relationships rear their ugly heads. Magdalena confesses that she had hoped that Jesus was in love with her to the prying attorneys and there's an initial, unrequited love between Edie and Dave that is finally happily resolved.

Key Moment(s): On numerous occasions in the film Hartley disrupts the fictive dream by having Satan address a microphone. This occurs first when Satan enters a bathroom and confronts the audience with the gleeful 'one more soul snatched away from the knowingly unknowable is still another feather in my cap.' During his pursuit of Jesus, Satan again comes across a microphone, mounted on a stand in the middle of the street. At first passing it, he returns to again speak directly to the audience, declaring, 'I can't give up now, I've come too close.' Both moments create and sustain tension but they also directly draw reference to the fact that we are watching an artificial creation in which actors act and speak their lines.

Similarly, in a black and white, apparently improvised scene in which Satan, Edie and Dave discuss the soup Edie is preparing for the homeless, the presence of a camera and a cameraman is readily acknowledged. All three actors directly address it until Dave, gradually realising the folly of selling Edie's soul, implores the cameraman to turn his camera off, placing his hand over the lens.

The above episodes are again evidence of the director's ability to mask limited finance with innovative, experimental methods and his desire to shake-up conventional viewing experiences and prescribed director/spectator relationships.

Music: Numerous artists were quick to offer original compositions for the film, notably Ben Watt, who had remained close friends since the Everything But The Girl promos, PJ Harvey and Yo La Tengo. The latter were rewarded for their many years of collaboration with a cameo role in the film as a Salvation Army Band.

Paying characteristic attention to the choice of songs and the ways in which they can contribute to the material, Hartley was keen to allow the music to affect both his writing and his directing, claiming that 'it conditioned my response to certain environments and actors' movements.' (49) This statement seems especially true of some of the longer, drum and bass pieces that accompany the hurried street scenes and the moments when Jesus stops to ponder the consequence of his actions. In regard to latter such moments David Byrne's *Machu Pichu* and Yo La Tengo's utterly transcendent *Turtle Soup* are especially well used. Compositions from Osnabrücker Jugend Choro and Le Mystere Des Voix Bulgares create the requisite sepulchral tone.

There are less original Hal Hartley compositions but the piece that acts as the backdrop for the chase sequence titled *Fugitive*, composed with Ryful is one of Hartley's strongest and most musically muscular creations.

Verdict: Undoubtedly one of Hartley's most vivid and purely and thrillingly enjoyable works, the film is impressive in its brevity, its high-wire combination of humour and sobriety and its firm grasp of the characteristics and possibilities of digital video technology. Whilst accurately reflecting the Millennial tension that hung heavy in the air as the year 1999 drew to a close, the engaging performances suggest that it was a pleasure to make. In her first and so far only screen venture, *PJ* Harvey emerges with credibility and in an expanded role from his upmarket goon in *Amateur* Dave Simonds is a hoot. Donovan makes a compulsive and strangely apt Jesus Christ, Jay Ryan a believable and at times pitiable Satan. Hartley maintains a perfect balance between an exploration of form and the sustaining of a more or less linear and certainly engrossing narrative, and on this evidence working within exact parameters is no bad thing for the director. 5/5.

No Such Thing (2001)

Cast: Sarah Polley (Beatrice), Robert Jóhn Burke (The Monster), Helen Mirren (The Boss), Julie Christie (Doctor Anna), Baltasar Kormákur (Doctor Artaud).

Crew: Direction Hal Hartley, Screenplay Hal Hartley, Cinematography Michael Spiller, Production Design Arni Pall Jöhannsson, Music Hal Hartley, Editing Steve Hamilton, 98 minutes.

Story: A depressed, alcoholic, insomniac monster living in northernmost Iceland has grown very tired with his lot. Alive since the beginning of time and witness to the evolution of humankind, the monster's endless days are punctuated by brief visits to the nearby village to terrorise the locals who live in mortal fear of him. Having grown weary of 'the time it takes to kill these idiots,' the monster nonetheless savagely devours a visiting TV crew, flinging their bones to the rocks below. However, before his grisly demise, one of the crew, Jim, manages to post a tape detailing the existence of the monster back to the unscrupulous boss of the New York based news television station where he worked.

During a departmental meeting to discuss which gory news story should be the lead piece, the tape is intercepted by Jim's fiancée Beatrice, an underling at the station. The boss senses an exploitable human-interest angle to the story and dispatches Beatrice to Reykjavik; however, due to terrorist activities Beatrice's plane is re-routed and later suffers a technical fault, causing it to plummet into the ocean. Miraculously surviving, Beatrice's body is found by an Icelandic trawler and she is delivered into the care of Doctor Anna. Her spinal injuries are extensive and Beatrice is forced to undergo a series of intense and painful operations. Spurning the offer of her boss to recount her experiences of survival, six whole months pass before Beatrice is allowed to continue her quest to find out what happened to her fiancé.

At the final village before the monster's lair, the locals who ply her with the local brew treat Beatrice with kindness and generosity. The next morning however Beatrice awakens on the monster's island and is confronted by a somewhat disheveled but nonetheless monstrous creature that reveals that the locals have offered her as a sacrifice. Though dismissive of Beatrice's inherent goodness, the monster refrains from ripping her head off in exchange that she helps him find the brilliant scientist Dr. Artaud, the one man who holds the key to the monster's indestructibility. After revealing the last resting place of Jim and convincing Beatrice of his suffering, the monster persuades Beatrice to help him but must also promise not to kill anybody on their journey back to New York, a journey that Beatrice unwisely decides would be better taken with the help of her former boss.

Arriving back in NYC, Beatrice and the monster are immediately at the centre of a media frenzy instigated by the wily, conniving TV boss who has made a promise to Beatrice to locate Dr. Artaud in return for an exclusive on the story. However, the boss soon reneges on her deal. Initially seduced by the attention she commands, Beatrice soon realises the extent of the monster's suffering and after witnessing his attack at the hands of an unruly street mob tired of his news item status, she enlists the help of another TV station aide and some demolition workers to deliver the monster to Artaud and so end his eternal misery.

Background: Following the funding problems encountered on *Henry Fool*, Hartley found something of an unlikely benefactor in Executive Producer Francis Ford Coppola, whose American Zoetrope partly financed *No Such Thing*. Coppola is rumoured to be a longtime admirer of Hartley's work. Having sourced finance from foreign sources on *Flirt*, Hartley again enjoyed the benefit of oversees monies with the involvement of The Icelandic Film Corporation. As well as offering the director the opportunity to once more broaden his vistas in terms of both settings and an aesthetic approach to filming the physical environment, the financing also brought Hartley together with another important figure in contemporary filmmaking, the Icelandic director Fridrik Thór Fridriksson whose 1994 title *Cold Fever* was as idiosyncratic a road movie as they come. Fridriksson's work certainly displays sensibilities akin to Hartley's, namely an askew sense of character, a striking sense of composition and an irreverence for narrative convention.

The original title for the film was *Monster* but the director was forced to amend by the colossus that is Walt Disney who felt that the title conflicted with their plans to release the animated *Monsters Inc*. Hartley was somewhat incredulous and was quoted at the time as being surprised that such a multi-national corporation should have even registered, let alone felt threatened by his own modest picture. However, legal pressure won. The incident has parallels with the film in a moment in which the boss of the Fox-style TV station is unable to run a report concerning the fact that the Mayor of New York has sold Manhattan to an unnamed major studio because the same studio also owns the TV network. A perceptive moment that is critical of the abuse of corporate power, it also speaks volumes about the nefarious mechanisms operating within the American entertainment industry.

No Such Thing was screened at the 2001 Cannes Film Festival in *Un Certain Regard*. The screening continued the director's strong relationship with the festival and suggested, in Europe at least, the critical respect he was able to command. The reaction from the press however was little short of scathing, with even longtime supporters of Hartley's work expressing disappointment with the film. Perhaps as a result, the film was only released in the US in March 2002 and at the time of writing still has no UK distributor or terrestrial broadcast sale.

Style: In terms of scale and scope, *No Such Thing* must arguably be considered amongst Hartley's most ambitious projects. Though *Flirt* had taken him to Berlin and Tokyo and *Henry Fool* had seen him grappling both with a larger number of central characters and a more expansive narrative arc, not to mention the decline of contemporary American society, *No Such Thing* sees the director working with a host of 'star' performers, the sweeping Icelandic landscape and the complexities of special effects. It's not *Godzilla* and never aspires to achieve a state of the art synergy between what is real and what can be imagined but Hartley's monster is nonetheless of the horned, clawed and fire breathing variety. In one scene, the beast displays his mammoth strength and innate savagery by lifting a house from its awnings to reveal the terrorised inhabitants cowering inside. As one might expect, the use of special effects and make-up, fine as they are, are largely understated in order to clearly present the monster as 'other' but to never detract from the more serious consideration of the monster's internal suffering and the way in which he both demonises and is demonised by human kind.

In terms of structure and genre the director has previously personalised frameworks such as the western, the melodrama etc. With *No Such Thing* Hartley turns his attention to folklore, fairytales and popular mythology. The most overt reference is *Beauty And The Beast*, the beast of which Burke's monster clearly resembles in his frock coat and slightly dandified dress. Beatrice, a name rich in mythical connotations, finally sees beyond the monster's physical ugliness and his admittedly decreasing tendency towards brutality – he has after all eaten her fiancé but admits that he's 'not the monster I used to be' – to recognise his inner turmoil. The film also makes implicit reference to popular monster figures such as Frankenstein and Dracula and indeed of course to the horror genre. There are the fearful, sacrifice-offering local villagers and the horse-backed guide that will go no further. Dr. Artaud (named after the French playwright) is also one in a long line of brilliant but deranged movie scientists and it's also tempting to read the moment where Beatrice forces the monster to promise that he will not kill anyone when he enters society as a wry nod to the same vow taken by the futuristic android in *Terminator 2*. Typically, the film makes much of the monster's misanthropic humour: when confronted with Beatrice's Christian homilies the monster resignedly states, 'I can see this is going to be a disaster.' Suffice to say, *No Such Thing* doesn't take itself too seriously, something its Cannes detractors seem to have overlooked.

Retaining the use of voice-over narration previously explored in *The Book Of Life*, this time however the narrator – Beatrice – is female, *No Such Thing* shares many formal similarities with Hartley's previous work. There is an experimental approach to the relationship between sound and image, particularly evident in the final scene where a cacophony of noise accompanies the monster's destruction and of course an exactitude in terms of framing and composition. Evident of course in the New York sequences, which largely take place in sleek, modern office interiors, it becomes even more pronounced and invigorating in the Icelandic environment. Particularly impressive is the shot where a sedated Beatrice is transported via dinghy to the monster's island, a lone visible figure battling against the choppy seas as he rows away from the rugged cliffs out toward the open sea.

Again demonstrating his ability to positively respond to filming conditions and to look afresh at his surroundings, with the admittedly naturally dramatic and photogenic Iceland sequences Hartley and Spiller achieve some of their most beautiful images yet, suggesting how far he has moved away from the enclosed, dialogue driven milieu of his earlier features. Surrounded by mountain ranges and roads that meander far beyond the horizon, with the journey Beatrice undertakes by car with Doctor Anna, Hartley imbues the film with a visual quality that is epic in tone. This tone is matched by the representation of the rugged, unforgiving landscapes in which the villagers dwell. Filming in what appears to be a dormant power station of some sort for the interiors of the monster's unwelcoming home ('drinking helps' and so empty bottles act as the main source of decoration), Hartley uses characteristically oblique camera angles and adopts an expressionistic approach in terms of *mise-en-scene*. Darkly lit, the industrial walkways and thoroughfares are often illuminated by the embers of the flames that the monster has breathed into the empty oil drums. It's certainly one way of saving on the heating bills.

These interiors contrast not only with the beauty and naturalism of the Icelandic countryside but also with the corporate and austere New York interior settings, which are dominated by artificial lighting and mirrors and glass. Of course the New York streets are captured in all their ragged glory: garbage pails, traffic, general hubbub and all, with the combined effect being the suggestion of a culture and general climate that is cold, clinical and, as the various catastrophic elements suggest, rapidly heading for meltdown. It is of course a violent world. At the start of the film Beatrice witnesses a bloody shoot-out at the airport and later, the monster suffers a vicious and humiliating street beating from various members of the public. In the same vein as the bawdy detailing of human bodily functions in *Henry Fool*, the monster's final indignity is to be urinated upon. Physical pain is evident elsewhere in the film; particularly in the suffering first Beatrice and then the monster must endure in order to achieve their respective cures. An attention to both medical and scientific practices is another preoccupation and *No Such Thing* contains in this regard a number of intricate visual sequences such as the shots of the contraption into which Beatrice is strapped and the overhead insert of the scraps of paper that constitute Artaud's theories concerning the transference of matter.

The jocularity of the film has already been touched upon but after considering the film's presentation of violence and suffering it is also worth noting that in this area too the director displays his customary wit and tendency to highlight the absurdity of sudden, petulant physical acts. When confronted by an old lady who chides him following one of his havoc wreaking forays to the village, the monster, who seems to act savagely because he is grouchy and moreover simply because it is expected of him, snaps her cane and tells her to 'fuck off.' Similarly, the director has fun with the monster's gruff disposition and with the kind of threats on-screen behemoths are expected to make. After failing to persuade Beatrice to help him find Artaud, the monster snaps, 'you'll help me out or I'm gonna come down there, bite your head off, tear your heart out and set the whole ugly mess on fire.'

Subtext: 'What would the world be like without monsters...We talk things into reality to convince ourselves they exist,' exclaims Dr. Artaud at one point, highlighting the film's concern with demonisation. Hartley's monster is largely metaphorical, a repository for human fears and insecurities, an allegorical creation afflicted with all too human characteristics such as self-loathing, a capacity for destruction and a tendency to drink too much. In his Icelandic habitat the monster commands fear from the local villagers who offer sacrifices to him as an act of self-preservation. On the streets of New York however and robbed of his mythology by the parasitical media, the monster presents less of a threat to society raised on more tangible elements such as terrorist warfare. In short, the monster is far less fearsome than the horrors already present in a civilization seemingly hell-bent on destruction. No wonder that there is a general lack of interest from the news team in finding out if the monster really exists and we should not forget that a grieving Beatrice is only allowed to travel to Iceland by her boss because 'we need to do these human interest stories from time to time.' Right to the end in fact the boss doubts the monster's authenticity, ascribing his condition to genetic modification.

No Such Thing shares the despairing worldview offered in *Henry Fool*. The monster may struggle against his darker impulses but humans have long since given into them. In a meeting to discuss possible lead stories for the day, the ethics of the news program in question being firmly founded on the 'if it bleeds it leads variety,' it emerges that the President has tried to kill himself, there are governmental strikes, economic collapse in Japan and emerging evidence that bootleg nuclear arms are being sold to both Pakistan and India. If this were not dispiriting enough, Beatrice's journey to the air-port is delayed by terrorists blowing up the bridges to the city and the release of nerve gas onto the subway by a religious group. Post-September 11th, the attentiveness to these issues seem eerily portentous and mindful of global instability and Anti-American sensibilities. As Beatrice, quoting her mother eloquently puts it, 'the world is a dangerous and uncertain place, a few moments here and there of selflessness and reflection are about as good as it gets.'

During her first confrontation with the monster the angelic Beatrice, whose survival of the plane crash leads to Doctor Anna's proclamation that she is 'blessed,' enters into a discourse on religion (a prominent subject) and the Christian teachings of forgiveness. The monster is not convinced and offers his own account of the evolution of humanity, even positing his own theory that he may in fact be God; either way, 'he's still fucked.' Describing how he cheered the human race on as it oozed from the slime and express-ing his disappointment with it, he bemoans having to endure 'humanity's victory over all things without even the option of killing myself.' Indiscrim-inately slaughtering human beings provided initial relief until the time and effort involved in offing what are described as 'idiots' became simply 'depressing.'

As well as offering a fairly thorough consideration of the roles played by medicine and science in shaping our existence, the film again continues Hartley's pervasive interest in the trust that underpins any human relation-ship. Central is the dynamic between Beatrice and the monster; she trusts him not to kill anybody, he trusts her to lead him to Artaud. Trust, of the misplaced variety, also binds Beatrice and her unscrupulous boss, who in her demonic demeanour is actually far more monstrous than the monster of the film. The boss manipulates her charge, understanding that she is 'well adjusted, optimistic, completely out of touch and will do anything we want. ' Ultimately however, Beatrice's experiences have toughened her up and she is able to turn the tables and sneak the monster out from under her boss's nose. Arrested for precipitating a potential world crisis after allowing the monster to escape, the reaction of the boss is to simply think up another news angle for her arrest, 'the demonisation of the media.'

As is probably clear, Hartley gives the media short shrift in the film. Depicting them as entirely without morals when it comes to the presentation of news and criticising their tendency to build up a figure or story to then deflate and abandon it once public interest wanes. The boss acts with a flagrant lack of sensitivity and a complete disregard to human feeling as evidenced by her reaction on hearing that a plane has crashed into the ocean: 'let's have a camera in the home of every parent to capture the suffering.' It is this presenting of human suffering as cheap entertainment that is perhaps at the heart of Hartley's barbed depiction of media-types. The director shows how the glitzy parties and the glamour can prove seductive and it is when Beatrice herself becomes a news item that she momentarily abandons her principles, donning figure-hugging dresses, quaffing champagne and indulging in one night stands with pretty but vacuous young guys. There is also the sense of disgust for the way in which the public consumes the media's sensationalist approach to covering events. When the boss proclaims, 'there's a world of bad news out there and all we need to do is get our hands on the very worse of it,' she does so in the knowledge that there's a baying, gang-mentality public ready to voraciously consume it.

Key Moment: After undergoing lengthy and painful operations to repair her injuries, Beatrice is finally discharged from hospital six months (an intertitle informs us) after first being admitted. Supported by Doctor Anna, Beatrice, shot from above, emerges somewhat uncertainly into the light. News of her miraculous survival has spread and there to greet her is a throng of children. As a visibly awed Beatrice tentatively begins to descend the hospital steps the children gently reach out and caress her hair, their hands lingering lovingly upon it. No words are exchanged during the scene, which simply takes place to a gentle accompaniment of chime-led, soothing music.

It's a relatively brief moment that is somewhat at odds both with the majority of the film and perhaps with Hartley's style in general. It certainly contains transcendental, even spiritual qualities and in the context of the narrative suggests both Beatrice's 'blessed' state and her symbolic representation of regeneration, hope and kindness. It's a scene of understated import and beauty.

Music: Working solely under his own name, the music on the film initially most closely resembles the score for *Amateur*, which also seemingly acted as inspiration for the design of the opening title sequences. Again erring towards classical influences, the opening piece retains the sounds of string instruments such as cellos and violins and is a sophisticated and 'serious' piece of tone-setting composition.

Perhaps the most eclectic music in the film, which notably largely eschews the use of tracks by other artists, is in the sequences where Beatrice travels through the Icelandic countryside. To complement the visual splendor of meandering roads that pass between towering mountain ranges and shots of the expansive, rugged Icelandic countryside, Hartley's tranquil, elegiac compositions rekindle the work of Werner Herzog's regular composer, Popul Vuh. Suitably, Vuh's score for Herzog's *Nosferatu* comes most readily to mind.

By contrast and acting as further evidence of Hartley's awareness of music's utility to prompt and replicate the visual tone, the music in the scenes where Beatrice and the monster return to the mean streets of New York is faster paced and more recognisably rhythmic. Echoing the track *Frantic* memorably used in *The Book Of Life*, harsher drum and guitar sounds are introduced to give a suitably, edgy, urban feel.

Verdict: The negative press the film received in Cannes overlooks its virtues, not least its visual beauty, its ambitious scope and its attempts to not only give an idiosyncratic take on mythology and horror but to contextualise them within the current social and political climate. Ultimately rather moving in its consideration of the monster's plight, it also contains flashes of Hartley's funny but deceptively sharp dialogue. Some of the performances jar a little and Polley, so vibrant in *The Sweet Hereafter* seems especially flat and one can't help but conclude that Hartley feels more comfortable working with his regular performers, many of whom (Bill Sage, James Urbaniak, Damian Young) appear here in 'cameo' roles. There are also moments when the material feels a little uneven as if there may have been creative interferences along the way and that Hartley was forced to adapt to considerations imposed upon him. Rumours of interference from

Coppola would seem to corroborate and the underlying sense is that *No Such Thing*, entertaining and interesting as it is, does not perhaps have the full confidence and surety of a Hal Hartley movie. 3/5.

Reference Materials

Note: The numbers in brackets below each source listed corresponds to those in the text to indicate sources from where quotes are taken.

Books

American Independent Cinema: A Sight And Sound Reader edited by Jim Hillier, UK, BFI Publishing, 2001, 12.99, ISBN 0851707599. Features an interesting *Henry Fool* article by Ryan Gilbey.

The Wallflower Critical Guide To Contemporary North American Directors edited by Yoram Allon, Del Cullen and Hannah Patterson, UK, Wallflower Press, 2000, 17.99, ISBN 1903364094. The Hartley entry offers a concise career summation.

Spike Mike Slackers & Dykes: A Guided Tour Across A Decade Of Independent American Cinema by John Pierson, UK, Faber & Faber, 1996, 12.99, ISBN 0571179142.

Stranger Than Paradise: Maverick Film-Makers In Recent American Cinema by Geoff Andrew, UK, Prion Books Limited, 1998, 16.99, ISBN 1853752746. One of the first UK critics to champion Hartley's work, *Time Out's* Geoff Andrew proved critical in helping Hartley's films reach wider audiences. Manages to be perceptive, affectionate and objective. (20)

Screenplays

All the screenplays listed below (minus that for *Surviving Desire*) include a Graham Fuller introduction and an incisive interview with the director. The resulting texts are illuminative and telling peeks into Hartley's methods and ambitions:

Henry Fool by Hal Hartley, UK, Faber & Faber, 1998, ISBN 0571195199. (33), (37), (38), (40), (42), (43), (44), (45)

Flirt by Hal Hartley, UK, Faber & Faber, 1996, 7.99, ISBN 057117954. (15), (16), (17), (27), (28), (29), (30), (31), (32), (34), (36)

Amateur by Hal Hartley, UK, Faber & Faber, 1994, 8.99, ISBN 057117213. (18), (19), (21), (22), (23), (24), (25), (26)

Surviving Desire (Knowing Is Not Enough), Projections 1 edited by John Boorman and Walter Donohue, UK, Faber & Faber, 1992, 9.99, ISBN 0571167292. (6), (9)

Simple Men And Trust by Hal Hartley, UK, Faber & Faber, 1992, 8.99, ISBN 0571167985. (1), (2), (3), (8), (10), (11), (12), (13), (14)

Other Significant Printed Materials

An excerpt from an interview between Hal Hartley and Kenneth Kaleta for the forthcoming *True Fiction Pictures, Hal Hartley In Conversation With Kenneth Kaleta.*

The Book Of Life Interview With Hal Hartley. A promotional page produced by sales agent Celluloid Dreams to accompany the *2000 Seen By* series. (46), (47), (48), (49)

Videos/DVDs

The Book Of Life, Fox Lorber, 2000, $19.80, DVD Region 1, ASIN B0000Y4DA.

Henry Fool, Columbia Tristar, 2001, 5.99, VHS PAL, ASIN B00004 CZ5Y.

Flirt, Artificial Eye, 1997, 15.99, VHS PAL, ASIN B00004CUUS

Amateur, Artificial Eye,1995, ,15.99, VHS PAL, ASIN B00004CQCE.

Three Shorts By Hal Hartley, Tartan Video, 1995, 15.99, VHS PAL, ASIN B00004COCL.

Simple Men, Tartan Video, 1994,15.99, VHS PAL

Trust, Tartan Video, 1994, 15.99, VHS PAL, ASIN B00004COCP.

The Unbelievable Truth, Anchor Bay Entertainment, 2001, $29.80, DVD Region 1, ASIN B000059PPA.

Other Related Video Works

Home Movies The Best Of Everything But The Girl, Warner Vision, 1993, 10.99, VHS Pal, ASIN B00004CNB6. Includes the video for *The Only Living Boy In New York*.

Trouble And Desire: An Interview With Hal Hartley, Ion Productions Ltd, 1998. A documentary featuring an exclusive interview filmed during the editing of *Henry Fool*. An edited version appears on the American DVD release of *The Unbelievable Truth*. (3), (5), (7), (35), (39), (41)

Made In The USA, 1991, Lucida Productions. Documentary produced for Channel Four in which Hartley, amongst others, discusses the tribulations of independent production.

Websites

www.possiblefilms.com - Comprehensive site produced by Hartley's production company.

us.imdb.com/Name?Hartley,+Hal

drumz.best.vwh.net/Hartley/

www.bbc.co.uk/films/2001/03/15/hal_hartley_career_profile_article.shtml

Soundtracks

The Book Of Life, Echostatic, 1999, $16.99. ASIN B00000JNMI. *Music From The Films Of Hal Hartley*, Echostatic, 1998, $14.90, ASIN B00000AZX1. Wonderful compilation that draws together music from the first three features plus tracks featured in *Surviving Desire* and *Theory of Achievement*.

Henry Fool, Echostatic, 1997, $16.99, ASIN B0000075QW.

Flirt, Echostatic, 1996, $14.90, ASIN B000003KX1.

Amateur, Matador, 1994, $14.22, ASIN B00000649A.

The Essential Library: Currently Available

Film Directors:

Woody Allen (2nd)	Tim Burton	Ang Lee
Jane Campion*	John Carpenter	Joel & Ethan Coen (2nd)
Jackie Chan	Steven Soderbergh	Clint Eastwood
David Cronenberg	Terry Gilliam*	Michael Mann
Alfred Hitchcock (2nd)	Krzysztof Kieslowski*	Roman Polanski
Stanley Kubrick (2nd)	Sergio Leone	Oliver Stone
David Lynch (2nd)	Brian De Palma*	George Lucas
Sam Peckinpah*	Ridley Scott (2nd)	James Cameron
Orson Welles (2nd)	Billy Wilder	Roger Corman
Steven Spielberg	Mike Hodges	Spike Lee
Hal Hartley		

Film Genres:

Blaxploitation Films	Bollywood	French New Wave
Horror Films	Spaghetti Westerns	Vietnam War Movies
Slasher Movies	Film Noir	Hammer Films
Vampire Films*	Heroic Bloodshed*	Carry On Films
German Expressionist Films		

Film Subjects:

Laurel & Hardy	Marx Brothers	Film Music
Steve McQueen*	Marilyn Monroe	The Oscars® (2nd)
Filming On A Microbudget	Bruce Lee	Writing A Screenplay
Film Studies		

Music:

The Madchester Scene	Beastie Boys	Jethro Tull
How To Succeed In The Music Business		The Beatles

Literature:

Cyberpunk	Philip K Dick	The Beat Generation
Agatha Christie	Sherlock Holmes	Noir Fiction
Terry Pratchett	Hitchhiker's Guide (2nd)	Alan Moore
William Shakespeare	Creative Writing	Tintin
Georges Simenon		

Ideas:

Conspiracy Theories	Nietzsche	UFOs
Feminism	Freud & Psychoanalysis	Bisexuality

History:

Alchemy & Alchemists	The Crusades	The Black Death
Jack The Ripper	The Rise Of New Labour	Ancient Greece
American Civil War	American Indian Wars	Witchcraft
Globalisation	Who Shot JFK?	

Miscellaneous:

Stock Market Essentials	How To Succeed As A Sports Agent	Doctor Who
Classic Radio Comedy		

Available at bookstores or send a cheque (payable to 'Oldcastle Books') to: **Pocket Essentials (Dept HH), P O Box 394, Harpenden, Herts, AL5 1XJ, UK.** £3.99 each (£2.99 if marked with an *). For each book add 50p(UK)/£1 (elsewhere) postage & packing